RAND NATIONAL DEFENSE RESEARCH INSTITUTE

T0122834

Training Cyber Warriors

What Can Be Learned from Defense Language Training?

Jennifer J. Li, Lindsay Daugherty

Prepared for the Office of the Secretary of Defense

For more information on this publication, visit www.rand.org/t/rr476

Library of Congress Control Number: 2015935309

ISBN: 978-0-8330-8728-7

Published by the RAND Corporation, Santa Monica, Calif.

© Copyright 2015 RAND Corporation

RAND® is a registered trademark.

www.rand.org

Preface

Over the past decade, cyber operations have become an increasingly important part of U.S. and international military capabilities. Research and the popular press note the rising threat from cyber warfare, including threats to military and federal government networks, as well as potential attacks on the U.S. economy, infrastructure, and business. To respond to this threat, cyber defense spending is projected to grow substantially—even while overall Pentagon spending is reduced. As the importance of cyber operations in national security grows, the U.S. military's ability to train individuals in cyber skills and ensure a robust cyber workforce becomes increasingly important in protecting the nation. There has been a particular focus on the need for cyber warriors—highly trained and specialized individuals who engage in offensive and defensive cyber warfare.

One field that might provide informative lessons to the Office of the Secretary of Defense and the services as they develop training to build the cyber warrior workforce is defense language training. Language training for U.S. national security took on heightened importance during World War II and has grown steadily since that time. While there is no perfect analogy between cyber warriors and another segment of the national security workforce, a number of similarities exist between the need for language skills and cyber expertise, including the need for a highly specialized skill that requires extensive training, the critical role of the skill in mission effectiveness, a need to quickly build capacity, and a potentially limited pipeline of qualified candidates.

In this exploratory study, we examine what the military services and national security agencies have done to train linguists—personnel with skills in critical languages other than English—and the kinds of language training provided to build and maintain this segment of the workforce. We draw from published documents, research literature, and interviews of experts in both language and cyber. We use this information to identify key considerations for government efforts to develop efficient and effective training approaches for cyber warriors. Given the small scope of this effort, we focus specifically on training, rather than the larger and more complex topic of workforce management, which we acknowledge is critically important.

This report should be of interest to those interested in training for the U.S. cyber defense workforce, as well as policymakers interested in cyber defense workforce management. It could also be of interest to those seeking an overview of defense language training.

This research was conducted within the Forces and Resources Policy Center of the RAND National Defense Research Institute, a federally funded research and development center sponsored by the Office of the Secretary of Defense, the Joint Staff, the Unified Combatant Commands, the Navy, the Marine Corps, the defense agencies, and the defense Intelligence Community.

For more information on the RAND Forces and Resources Policy Center, see http:/www.rand.org/nsrd/ndri/centers/frp.html, or contact the director (contact information is provided on the web page).

Contents

Figure

Summary

Recent reports note the rising threat from cyber warfare, including threats to the computer networks of the U.S. military, government, infrastructure, and businesses.[1] To respond to this threat, cyber defense spending is projected to grow to $4.7 billion under President Obama's 2014 budget—an increase of $800 million.[2] As the role of cyber operations in national security grows, the U.S. military's ability to ensure a robust cyber workforce is increasingly important. A particular concern has been the growing need for cyber warriors—highly trained and specialized individuals who engage in offensive and defensive operations. As part of its workforce management efforts, the U.S. Department of Defense (DoD) may need to develop additional training approaches at the same time that it plans for broader recruiting and workforce management to ensure sufficient numbers of skilled cyber warriors.

In this paper, we focus specifically on training and seek to help those planning future cyber training by highlighting what can be learned from another specialty—defense language. Although there is no perfect analogy between cyber warriors and another specialty, we believe that some of the similarities between the two fields—such as the need for specialized training, role in mission preparedness, need to increase capacity quickly, and potentially limited pipeline—make les-

---

[1] For example, see James R. Clapper, Director of National Intelligence, "Worldwide Threat Assessment of the U.S. Intelligence Community," Statement for the Record: House Permanent Select Committee on Intelligence, April 11, 2013; and Defense Science Board, "Resilient Military Systems and the Advanced Cyber Threat," Task Force Report, January 2013.

[2] Jim Michaels, "Pentagon Expands Cyber-Attack Capability," *USA Today*, April 23, 2013.

sons from language potentially valuable for cyber. For these reasons, we investigated the high-level lessons that language training could offer cyber training.

Approach

This report documents the results of a modest exploratory effort to identify potential lessons from defense language training to inform the planning of training for the cyber defense workforce. We sought to answer the following questions:

- What is the current state of the U.S. cyber defense workforce and training?
- What aspects of defense language training are viewed as successful, and which areas remain challenging?
- What key issues should be considered in planning training to expand the U.S. cyber warrior workforce?
- What preliminary lessons can be drawn from U.S. defense language training?

To carry out this effort, we reviewed relevant literature, conducted interviews with cyber and language experts, and consulted documents on training in each field. Interviewees included leaders from DoD offices, officials from the Intelligence Community, individuals involved with the management and oversight of education and training programs, and experts from postsecondary education institutions. From the interviews, we identified the topics most commonly cited as important for establishing an effective and efficient training strategy. We developed a framework to organize these topics, and we used the framework to guide our discussion of key considerations for the buildup of cyber warrior training and the lessons learned from defense language training.

Overview of Cyber Workforce Needs and Cyber Warrior Training

While this study focuses on cyber warriors, the most highly specialized group of individuals involved in offensive and defensive cyber warfare, the cyber workforce is much larger. A 2011 DoD report describes a cyber workforce of more than 160,000 military and civilian personnel, more than 5 percent of the DoD workforce.[3] The experts we interviewed reported that there is no clear understanding of the capabilities needed in the cyber workforce or cyber warrior workforce and the individuals who are currently serving in roles that meet these needs. Without understanding the existing resources available to meet these capabilities and the additional knowledge, skills, and abilities that are intended to be developed through training, it is difficult to develop an effective training strategy.

Rapid Growth in Demand for Cyber Warriors

General Keith Alexander (Ret.), who served as the commander of U.S. Cyber Command (CyberCom) from 2010 through early 2014, often focused attention on the cyber warrior workforce, calling for the addition of thousands of cyber warriors to support CyberCom by 2015.[4] Cyber warriors are highly trained individuals who engage in offensive and defensive warfare. The call for thousands of additional cyber warriors raised concerns about the ability to scale up the workforce quickly.[5] The services have made progress, but 2013 reports suggest that 3,700 more cyber warriors are needed, so training will need to

---

[3] Department of Defense, "Cyber Operations Personnel Report," Report to Congressional Defense Committees, April 2011b.

[4] General Keith B. Alexander (Ret.), Commander of United States Cyber Command, "Statement Before the Senate Committee on Armed Services," March 27, 2012; General Keith B. Alexander (Ret.), Commander of United States Cyber Command, "Statement Before the Senate Committee on Armed Services," March 12, 2013a; Zachary Fryer-Biggs, "DoD Still 3,700 Cyber Experts Short of Full Staff," *Defense News*, April 25, 2013.

[5] Tim Starks, "Facing Up to the Nation's Shortage of Cyber-Warriors," Roll Call, March 19, 2013; Defense Science Board, 2013; Jared Serbu, "DoD Building Cyber Workforce of the Future," Federal News Radio, September 9, 2012.

continue at accelerated levels and potentially be expanded to meet these needs.[6] In addition, the service-specific needs for cyber expertise are growing, so it is likely that the demand for cyber warriors for these missions will continue to increase as well.

Existing Training for Cyber Warriors

A range of training options currently exists for the training of cyber warriors. Below, we highlight those described by the cyber experts and cyber military resources we consulted.

Central/Joint Training

While initially a Navy course, the six-month Joint Cyber Analysis Course (JCAC) provided at the Navy's Correy Station base in Pensacola, Florida, is now used for cyber warrior training across all of the services.

Service-Specific Training

There is a range of efforts taking place within the services to train cyber warriors for service-specific operations and joint missions. The Air Force, Navy, Marine Corps, and Army each provide a range of courses in cyber operations, as well as on-the-job training, which can take three to five years.[7]

Colleges and Centers of Excellence

The Centers of Academic Excellence (CAEs) were established in 1999 to provide cyber education in information assurance. The number of CAEs expanded rapidly, from just seven in 1999 to 117 in 2011.[8]

Competitions and Outreach

DoD and the federal agencies have developed a range of competitions and outreach activities to provide real-life training opportunities and build the pipeline of potential cyber warriors. There are also hacking

---

[6]   Fryer-Biggs, 2013.

[7]   Joe Gould, "Army Ramps Up Cybersecurity Skills Training," *Army Times*, November 19, 2012.

[8]   DoD, 2011b.

competitions for high school cyber teams. The National Defense University's iCollege also conducts a range of outreach activities.

Industry

The experts we interviewed suggested that many of the training materials and methods currently in use initially came from industry. However, to the extent that DoD cyber operations may involve actions that are illegal in the civilian world, industry may be limited in what it can offer offensive operations.

Overview of Defense Language Training, Successes, and Challenges

Currently, many military personnel who will become language specialists must be trained from zero or from a very low skill level to become linguists or cryptologists; therefore, U.S. defense agencies provide substantial training to meet the need for language-skilled personnel. Below, we briefly describe U.S defense language training and summarize insights from interviews and the literature about successes and challenges in the field.

Delivery of Training for Defense Language Personnel

A range of training options exists for defense language personnel:

Language Training Institutes and Programs

The Defense Language Institute Foreign Language Center (DLIFLC) in Monterey, California, part of the U.S. Army Training and Doctrine Command, serves as a joint institute for students from the Army, Navy, Air Force, Marines, and other agencies. In addition, the National Cryptologic School, Foreign Service Institute, and CIA University, among others, each train students for specific purposes. Other agencies—such as U.S. Special Operations Command and the U.S. Air Force, Navy, and Marines—also provide specialized, mission-specific language training to selected personnel.

College- and University-Based Programs

Besides the institutes and programs described above, the services and other government agencies take advantage of college- and university-based language programs. In addition, DoD has established partnerships such as the Language Flagship, Project GO, and the Language Training Centers, which provide training opportunities designed to produce advanced capabilities in languages critical to U.S. national security.[9] At the time of this report, there were 26 university Language Flagship programs, 22 Project GO programs, and five Language Training Centers.

Commercial and Contract Language Training Providers

A good deal of language training takes place through outside providers, such as Berlitz and Inlingua, or via small business language training organizations. They provide a variety of services, including group instruction, distance learning, and one-on-one tutoring.

Pipeline-Building Programs

The Language Flagship initiative (described above), which provides funding for advanced language training at universities, also includes funding for K–12 education to address the early years of students' education and build the pipeline of second-language–proficient individuals in the U.S. workforce.

Successes and Challenges in Language Training

Interviewees highlighted a number of areas in which they view the current system of language training as working well:

- *Training has been tailored to a variety of needs.* Interviewees noted that the existing training programs meet a wide variety of different needs, such as training for certain types of skills and to specified levels of proficiency.
- *Screening tools have been created to identify candidates who are more likely to succeed.* The experts we interviewed cited the ability to screen candidates and select the most promising as a mechanism

---

[9]   Language Flagship, home page, 2013.

that makes training more efficient by reducing attrition, thus reducing wasted resources.

- *The field has shared definitions and metrics.* The Interagency Language Roundtable scale and skill-level descriptions give those providing training, measuring skills, and employing skilled personnel a shared understanding of training goals and outcomes.
- *The range of training options meets the diverse needs of many stakeholders.* Although interviewees noted the system's shortcomings, they pointed out that it accommodates a wide range of needs and is able to respond to emerging demands for specific languages.
- *Agencies have access to a joint training resource.* Some experts commented that the existence of a joint training institute, such as DLIFLC, offered advantages because it provided a single source for basic language and culture training and relieved individual agencies from having to duplicate one another's efforts.

The experts we interviewed also noted a number of areas in which defense language training faces challenges:

- *The pipeline of skilled personnel is limited.* Several of the language experts interviewed cited a limited pipeline of language-skilled personnel as an ongoing challenge to the field.
- *Training to high levels of proficiency is time consuming.* Some of those we interviewed expressed the view that existing programs take too long.
- *Institutions rarely share resources.* The existing institutions were described by some experts as rarely sharing resources—perhaps due to the rapid pace of their work—thus missing opportunities to leverage the expertise of other organizations.
- *Most university-based training is regarded as inadequate.* With the exception of the Language Flagship universities and a few others, the interviewees pointed to weak language instruction and a lack of practical orientation by many university language programs.
- *Concerns remain about cost and return on investment.* Because the cost of language training is high, interviewees expressed concerns

about the retention rates of those who receive training and the return on investment.

Key Considerations for Developing an Effective Training Strategy for Cyber Warriors

Through our expert interviews and the literature, we found that cyber and language training face similar issues, so we developed a framework to represent the overarching set of considerations that emerged in the interviews across both fields as recurring themes important to strategic training decisions. The framework highlights four key considerations:

- **What should the training look like?** To determine what the content and form of the training should be, it is important to identify the *knowledge, skills, and abilities* required for the job, as well as the *mission needs*; understand the *platforms/language* in which skills are needed; and identify the *best means for delivery* of training.
- **Who is being trained?** To clearly define who is being trained, an organization must assess the *workforce makeup* (e.g., military/civilian/contractor, active duty/reserves), determine how the *pipeline* will be developed, *screen individuals* to determine their abilities and potentially sort them into positions, and *determine the stage of skill development* to identify what an individual needs to learn for career progression.
- **What resources are needed?** The resources required to provide training should be balanced against the benefits of various delivery methods to ensure that training is delivered efficiently. We focus on several of the most critical resource requirements, including *level and payer of costs, infrastructure, staffing, management,* and *time required.*
- **How should the training be integrated into the larger picture of workforce management?** Training for highly skilled individuals can be resource intensive, so it is critical to ensure that there is a return on the investment in training. Key elements of the

bigger workforce picture that must be considered include *retention, workforce management, career paths,* and *continued training* for individuals who have been trained.

Preliminary Lessons from Language Training for Cyber Training

Based on an overview of cyber defense needs, the defense language training landscape, our literature review, and insights from experts in both language and cyber training, we identified several themes that policymakers and planners should consider for the training of cyber warriors.

- **Shared definitions, training standards, and metrics are an important first step in ensuring efficient training and workforce management.** They give diverse stakeholders the ability to share a common vernacular, set goals, and assess outcomes consistently. Defense language training benefits from established tools and metrics. In cyber, efforts are under way to establish shared definitions and metrics. When widely available, they will be important assets to those who plan and design training.
- **Close alignment with mission needs is important to effective training.** As in any domain of national security, mission needs may vary substantially. Those we interviewed consistently noted the need for training to be well matched to an individual's responsibilities in service to the mission, whether it is a joint or service-specific mission.
- **Training may benefit from a variety of training providers and delivery methods to enable responsiveness to diverse mission needs and diverse groups of trainees.** Defense language training comes from many sources, and the cyber experts we interviewed emphasized the advantages of distributed, modular training for some skills; in-person, on-the-job mentorship for others; and team-based training for others. Their comments point to the need for a variety of options to meet diverse needs.

- **Training individuals from a zero skill level is costly and often inefficient, so building a strong pipeline of candidates may be beneficial.** Experts in both fields pointed out that training demands are substantially reduced when candidates have existing expertise. Even though there may be a larger pipeline of individuals interested in cyber relative to language, the field may benefit greatly from efforts to cultivate the pipeline because it is less costly to train individual with preexisting skills.
- **Cyber training may benefit from the development of validated screening tools or processes that can be used across the field.** Interviewees from both language and cyber identified aptitude screening as important to identifying the most promising candidates. This may be critical in cyber, where the pool of individuals is larger, but those qualified to reach the highest levels of expertise may be a small proportion.
- **Alignment between workforce management priorities and training plans is important.** Because advanced skill training is costly and time consuming, those interviewed emphasized that cyber defense stakeholder agencies will benefit from workforce management policies that develop career paths and aid retention to maximize the return on investments in training.

Acknowledgments

We are grateful to the language and cyber professionals who participated in the interviews for this study. Without their candid input, we could not have conducted this research. We are also grateful to Beth Asch, James Hosek, Lara Schmidt, and Robert Slater, who provided valuable suggestions during the research. Finally, we thank our reviewers, Sarah Meadows and Martin Libicki, whose feedback substantially strengthened the report.

Abbreviations

ASVAB	Armed Services Vocational Aptitude Battery
CAE	Center of Academic Excellence
CAPE	Cost Assessment and Program Evaluation
CBO	Congressional Budget Office
CIA	Central Intelligence Agency
CyberCom	U.S. Cyber Command
DLAB	Defense Language Aptitude Battery
DLI	Defense Language Institute
DLIFLC	Defense Language Institute Foreign Language Center
DLPT	Defense Language Placement Test
DoD	U.S. Department of Defense
FSI	Foreign Service Institute
GAO	U.S. Government Accountability Office
IT	information technology
JCAC	Joint Cyber Analysis Course
JIE	Joint Information Environment
KSAs	knowledge, skills, and abilities

NICE   National Initiative for Cybersecurity Education

NSA   National Security Agency

STEM   science, technology, engineering, and mathematics

CHAPTER ONE

Introduction

Over the past decade, cyber operations have become an increasingly important part of U.S. and international military capabilities. Recent reports note the rising threat from cyber warfare—armed conflicts conducted wholly or partially in cyber space—including threats to networks for the military and federal government, as well as potential attacks on the U.S. economy, infrastructure, and business.[1] To respond to this threat, cyber defense spending is projected to grow to $4.7 billion under President Obama's 2014 budget—an increase of $800 million—while overall Pentagon spending is cut by $3.9 billion.[2] As the importance of cyber operations in national security grows, the U.S. military's ability to ensure a robust cyber workforce becomes increasingly important in protecting the nation. One of the five major initiatives in U.S. Department of Defense (DoD) cyber strategy is to "leverage the nation's ingenuity through an exceptional cyber workforce and rapid technological innovation."[3] According to this strategy document, "The development and retention of an exceptional cyber workforce is central to DoD's strategic success." As part of its workforce management efforts, DoD may need to develop additional training approaches at the same time that it plans for broader recruiting and

---

[1] For example, see James R. Clapper, Director of National Intelligence, "Worldwide Threat Assessment of the U.S. Intelligence Community," Statement for the Record: House Permanent Select Committee on Intelligence, April 11, 2013; and Defense Science Board, "Resilient Military Systems and the Advanced Cyber Threat," Task Force Report, January 2013.

[2] Jim Michaels, "Pentagon Expands Cyber-Attack Capability," *USA Today*, April 23, 2013.

[3] Department of Defense, "Strategy for Operating in Cyberspace," January 2011a.

workforce management to ensure sufficient numbers of skilled cyber workers.

In this report, we focus specifically on training and seek to help those planning future cyber training by highlighting what can be learned from training for another specialty—defense language. Language skills for national security took on heightened importance during World War II[4] and have received ongoing attention by the military and intelligence agencies since that time. In August 2011, then–Secretary of Defense Leon Panetta underscored the importance of language, regional expertise, and culture as enduring warfighting competencies.[5] Although there is no perfect analogy between cyber and another defense specialty, we believe that some of the similarities between the two fields make lessons from language potentially valuable for cyber. Both are specialized skills that require training, which may be extensive for certain jobs. Both are viewed by military leaders as critical to mission preparedness. Both have faced a need to increase capacity quickly—language in the World War II era and again more recently in the Middle East conflicts, and cyber in recent years and the present. And both have potentially limited pipelines of individuals who have the advanced skills required. For these reasons, we investigated the high-level lessons that language training could offer cyber training.

A Pressing Need for Cyber Warriors

While there are likely to be increasing workforce needs and thus training needs across the cyber sector, *cyber warriors*—individuals engaged in offensive and defensive cyber operations—have been a population of particular focus. In recent speeches, General Keith Alexander (Ret.), who served as the commander of U.S. Cyber Command (CyberCom) from 2010 through early 2014, often focused attention on the cyber warrior workforce, calling for the addition of thousands of cyber war-

---

[4]   U.S. Army Garrison Presidio of Monterey, "History of the Defense Language Institute Foreign Language Center," last updated January 10, 2013.

[5]   Leon Panetta, Memorandum, OSD 09206-11, August 10, 2011.

riors to support CyberCom by 2015.[6] A recent report by the Defense Science Board discusses the importance of building the cyber warrior workforce, and a number of articles in military publications document the growing need for these highly trained individuals to support cyber warfare operations.[7] About the need for cybersecurity professionals, Air Force Chief Information Officer Lt. Gen. Michael Basla is quoted as saying, "Do we have enough? Probably not today, based on what we've forecasted for the demand tomorrow" and "It's a big job in front of us, with a lot of attention on it right now."[8]

Cyber warriors are expected to defend networks and/or use complex cyber weapon systems, so they typically require extensive training beyond what is provided to the average military or civilian worker in the same field.[9] There is a concern that these substantial training requirements and the rapid scaling up of the workforce will lead to challenges meeting workforce needs.[10] In this report, we seek to help those planning future training for cyber warriors by identifying lessons learned from another specialty—language.

For these reasons, we examine training specifically, understanding that meeting needs for a high-quality cyber warrior workforce involves other aspects of workforce management, including recruitment and hiring, placement, compensation, and retention. We also

---

[6] General Keith B. Alexander (Ret.), commander of United States Cyber Command, "Statement Before the Senate Committee on Armed Services," March 27, 2012; General Keith B. Alexander (Ret.), commander of United States Cyber Command, "Statement Before the Senate Committee on Armed Services," March 12, 2013a; Zachary Fryer-Biggs, "DoD Still 3,700 Cyber Experts Short of Full Staff," *Defense News*, April 25, 2013.

[7] Defense Science Board, 2013.

[8] A. Corrin, "Is There a Cybersecurity Workforce Crisis?" FCW, October 15, 2013.

[9] An expert interviewee from the Air Force described four to six years of preparation and training for a new enlistee to become a highly skilled cyber warrior, including three or four years of on-the-job training to build basic cyber and military skills and screen for the most highly qualified individuals, followed by at least one to two years of advanced training.

[10] Tim Starks, "Facing Up to the Nation's Shortage of Cyber-Warriors," *Roll Call*, March 19, 2013; Defense Science Board, 2013; Jared Serbu, "DoD Building Cyber Workforce of the Future," Federal News Radio, September 9, 2012.

discuss how other aspects of workforce management may influence training decisionmaking.

The Potential to Learn from Other Highly Specialized Fields

This study was undertaken to determine the value of drawing comparisons across fields to ensure that training is developed in a way that is as effective and efficient as possible. We examine what the military services and national security agencies have done to meet the need for linguists—personnel with skills in critical languages other than English—and the language training provided to build and maintain this segment of the workforce. We use this information to identify key considerations for government efforts to develop efficient and effective training approaches for cyber warriors. We selected defense language training as the reference point for this exploratory study because of a number of similarities between the two fields, including the need for a highly specialized skill that requires extensive training, the critical role of the skill in mission effectiveness, a need to quickly build capacity, and a potentially limited pipeline of qualified individuals to fill positions in the short term.

It is important to note, however, that key differences exist between the fields of language and cyber that may lead to different conclusions about the way to best train each workforce, and we do not suggest a perfect analogy between the fields. For example, it is widely acknowledged that knowledge and skills in the cyber field evolve more quickly than those for language. Further, language is not the only field that might offer lessons to cyber defense training. Other fields that may offer lessons in to the cyber sector include special operations, health care, and master craftsmanship fields. In particular, fields that have well-established training strategies and those that face challenges similar to those encountered in the cyber environment can provide important lessons on what is most important to consider in developing training, what has worked well in training highly specialized workforces, and where DoD has faced challenges in designing and delivering the training.

Our Approach to Exploring Lessons Learned

This paper reports on a modest exploratory effort to focus specifically on training needs and identify potential lessons from defense language training to inform the planning of training for the cyber defense workforce. We sought to answer the following questions:

- What is the current state of the U.S. cyber defense workforce and training?
- What aspects of defense language training are viewed as successful, and which areas remain challenging?
- What key issues should be considered in planning training to expand the U.S. cyber warrior workforce?
- What preliminary lessons can be drawn from U.S. defense language training?

To carry out this effort, we reviewed relevant literature and conducted interviews with a range of experts from the language and cyber fields. Interviewees included leadership within DoD offices, officials from the Intelligence Community, individuals involved with the management and oversight of education and training programs within DoD, and language and cyber experts from postsecondary education institutions. Each of the individuals had current or recent substantial involvement with policymaking, planning, and/or management of training in language and/or cyber. Two of the individuals interviewed had involvement with both fields. We interviewed seven experts in the defense language community about the primary methods of defense language training, successes in the field, and challenges. Similarly, we interviewed seven experts in the cyber defense community about current methods of training, with a focus on what is being done well and what needs refinement as CyberCom and the services work to meet workforce needs for cyber warfare. From the interviews, we identified common topics that were identified as important for establishing an effective and efficient training strategy. We present a framework to organize these topics, and we use the framework to guide our discussion of key considerations for the buildup of cyber warrior training and the lessons learned from defense language training.

To supplement our expert interviews, we consulted relevant documents and research on language and cyber training, including recent reports from DoD and the Government Accountability Office (GAO), U.S. Census data, transcripts of speeches given by cyber leadership, DoD memos, cyber strategy documents, documentation from language training providers, news articles on cyber and language training, and reports from research organizations. We also conducted a targeted review of information on the websites for CyberCom, service-specific cyber offices, the Defense Language and National Security Education Office, service-related language programs, DoD-funded language programs, and other government agencies that provide language training. In addition, to further our understanding of certain topics addressed in interviews, we conducted targeted searches on specific topics raised in our interviews (e.g., the Joint Cyber Analysis Course).

As an exploratory effort with limited scope, this study has some limitations. First, our data draw primarily from government and academic sources. A more expansive effort would explore private-sector perspectives on these issues as well. Second, the short duration of the study limited its depth and breadth. Third, while we acknowledge that training is a component of a larger workforce management strategy and discuss the need to consider other aspects of workforce management alongside training, we do not delve into this larger and more complex issue. Future efforts will benefit from additional time to examine the issues more deeply and collect data that represent perspectives from other specializations and sectors.

The rest of this report is organized as follows. In Chapter Two, we describe the cyber workforce and the increased need for cyber warriors. We also discuss the current approaches to training cyber warriors. Chapter Three describes some of the prominent components of defense language training currently in place, aspects of the field that are working well, and those that face challenges. In Chapter Four, we identify areas on which those designing training for cyber warriors should focus attention as they expand the workforce. We organize the discussion around a framework that outlines the major questions to address the development of a training strategy. Finally, in Chapter Five, we highlight the key themes that emerged in this exploratory study—considerations that may be useful to policymakers concerned with training the workforce of cyber warriors.

CHAPTER TWO

Understanding Cyber Workforce Needs and Cyber Warrior Training

Describing the Cyber Workforce

While this study focuses on cyber warriors, the most highly specialized group of individuals involved in offensive and defensive cyber warfare, the cyber workforce is actually much larger. A 2011 DoD report describes a cyber workforce of more than 160,000 military and civilian personnel, more than 5 percent of the DoD workforce.[1] The cyber workforce is very diverse and includes individuals providing basic information technology (IT) services, designing systems, protecting networks, and engaging in cyber warfare, among other activities.

A major concern within the cyber field has been the lack of clarity about how to characterize the cyber workforce. According to one article, DoD has released a wide range of counts for the size of the workforce, reporting 66,000 cybersecurity workers in a 2010 Office of Management and Budget report, 87,846 workers in a 2010 Federal Information Security Management Act report, 88,159 workers in a 2011 GAO data call, and 18,955 workers in a 2010 Office of Personnel Management study.[2] A U.S. Joint Forces Command report found that

---

[1] Department of Defense, "Cyber Operations Personnel Report," Report to Congressional Defense Committees, April 2011b.

[2] David J. Kay, Terry J. Pudas, and Brett Young, "Preparing the Pipeline: The U.S. Cyber Workforce for the Future," Institute for National Strategic Studies, August 2012.

the lack of common definitions around cyber and the lack of coordination across the services can lead to confusion in workforce planning.[3] Experts report that the cyber workforce is often categorized under the umbrella of intelligence, communication, or command and control, rather than having its own classification scheme. They also perceive substantial variation in the way that services identify and manage their cyber workforces. Without a clear picture of what capabilities are needed to successfully complete cyber missions and what job roles are required to meet these needs, it is difficult to develop an effective recruitment and training strategy. Given that public documentation on cyber missions and required capabilities is limited, we focus on the positions that are typically classified as part of the cyber workforce and the individuals who currently fill these positions.

In an attempt to better describe the cyber workforce and the job duties that these individuals perform, DoD's 2011 personnel report breaks the cyber workforce into three groups: operators and maintainers, information assurance, and defensive operations.[4] DoD defines defensive operations as "countermeasures designed to detect, identify, intercept, and destroy or negate harmful activities attempting to penetrate or attack through cyberspace."[5] At the time of the report, nearly 90 percent of the workforce was designated as operators and maintainers, while only 9 percent were considered as information assurance, and only 2 percent were working in defensive operations (3,777 individuals). However, even among these groups there is substantial overlap between information assurance and operation/maintenance, so the classification is not perfect. The report does not discuss positions in offensive warfare.

With regard to civilian/military mix, the 2011 DoD personnel report found that 78 percent of the cyber workforce involved in defen-

---

[3] U.S. Government Accountability Office, "DOD Faces Challenges In Its Cyber Activities," Washington, D.C., GAO-11-75, May 2011a.

[4] DoD, 2011b.

[5] DoD, "Joint Terminology for CyberSpace Operations," Memorandum for Chiefs of the Military Services, Commanders of the Combatant Commands, and Directors of the Joint Staff Directorates, 2010.

sive operations was civilian. However, other sources suggest a somewhat larger role of the military in cyber warfare. In 2012, the 24th
Air Force, the cyber operational wing, reported a population that was
24 percent active-duty personnel, 66 percent Reserve/Guard personnel,
and just 11 percent civilian or contractor personnel.[6] According to an
American Forces Press Service report, the Navy is aiming for a cyber
workforce that is 80 percent military and 20 percent civilian.[7] Our
expert interviewees described the most highly specialized cyber warriors as being primarily enlisted service members, with some involvement of officers in overseeing cyber missions, and a supporting role
for civilians. In offensive operations, the military plays a particularly
central role. Three of the services reported plans to only use active-duty
and reserve military personnel to conduct offensive cyberspace operations, as statutory authority requires offensive activities to be restricted
to the military.[8] A 2011 GAO report argued that there was a lack of
guidance around the role civilians and contractors should play in the
execution of cyber operations, so the role of civilians and contractors
remained limited.[9] Yet the services reported plans to expand the role of
the civilian workforce in offensive operations if military cyber capabilities were stretched and statutes were revised.

In addition to describing the makeup of the cyber workforce,
there are efforts to better define the type of work that is being done and
determine what the missions are. In 2009, U.S. Strategic Command
established CyberCom to oversee cyber operations and lead joint force
teams to fight national cyber risks. To further clarify how the Cyber-
Com workforce would be organized, General Alexander (Ret.) identified three groups of individuals: (1) a Cyber National Mission Force

[6]   Stew Magnuson, "Air Force Cyber-Operations Wing to Go on Hiring Binge," *National Defense Magazine*, January 17, 2013.

[7]   Cheryl Pellerin, "For Navy, Cyber Has Inherently Military Operational Aspect," *American Forces Press Service*, June 12, 2013.

[8]   GAO, 2011a; United States Code, Title 10, Volume 3, Armed Forces, 112th Congress, House of Representatives, July 2011.

[9]   GAO, "More Detailed Guidance Needed to Ensure Military Services Develop Appropriate Cyberspace Capabilities," Washington, D.C., GAO-11-421, May 2011b.

and teams to help defend the nation against national-level threats, (2) a Cyber Combat Mission Force with teams that will be assigned to the operational control of individual combatant commanders to support their objectives (pending resolution of the cyber command and control model by the Joint Staff), and (3) a Cyber Protection Force and teams to help operate and defend the DoD information environment.[10] In addition to serving joint needs, General Alexander (Ret.) argued that these teams would contribute to service-specific cyber needs. However, we heard concerns from experts about the potential for forces that are trained and/or managed at the central level to have a reduced focus on service-specific needs. They argue that separate cyber warrior work-forces are likely to be needed within the services to meet these distinct operational needs.

As DoD and CyberCom work to better define the workforce, there are also efforts to better define and describe the cyber workforce across federal agencies. The National Initiative for Cybersecurity Education (NICE), established in January 2008 by President George W. Bush, has developed a framework to describe the makeup of the federal cyber workforce, including the job roles that individuals hold; the tasks that are undertaken within these job roles; and the knowledge, skills, and abilities (KSAs) that are required to be successful in undertaking these tasks.[11] The NICE framework identifies seven specialty areas across which the cyber workforce is divided: securely provision, operate and maintain, protect and defend, investigate, collect and operate, analyze, and oversight and development.

Yet despite all of these efforts, the cyber experts we interviewed suggested that the lack of clarity around the makeup of the cyber workforce is a persistent issue, arguing that an important first step in developing training approaches that are effective and efficient will be to ensure a clear definition and understanding of the cyber warrior workforce. Without a clear and common way of defining and managing the workforce, it is difficult to identify potential gaps in workforce needs and assess whether training approaches and other workforce

---

[10]   Alexander, 2013a.

[11]   See NICE, homepage, 2014.

management efforts are helping to address those needs. CyberCom is currently working to create a common set of definitions, classifications, and standards to improve cyber workforce management.[12] In addition, we heard reports that some of the services are currently undertaking efforts to refine the management of their cyber workforces and classify workforce needs more systematically. For example, after the most recent Cyber Summit, the Air Force developed a more objective set of criteria to describe "the highly specialized cyber workforce." According to one expert, the following criteria are included: (1) Individuals must fall under a particular Air Force Specialty Code; (2) Individuals must have jobs that require a specialized skill set; and (3) Individuals must require an exceptional amount of training. According to one cyber expert, this definition classifies approximately 8 percent of the Air Force's 65,000 cyber workers as highly specialized cyber experts.

Rapid Growth in Demand for Cyber Warriors

As described in Chapter One, the role of cyber activities in DoD operations is growing. As cyber skills become more important to U.S. defense, the need to build a group of cyber warriors—highly specialized individuals involved in offensive and defensive cyber warfare—has become an issue of increasing focus. Several key cyber strategy documents emphasize the importance of cyber warriors in driving the success of operations. A 2013 Defense Science Board report recommends that DoD "increase the number of cyber warriors . . . [and] scale up efforts to recruit, provide facilities and training, and use these critical people effectively."[13]

The call for thousands of additional cyber warriors by 2015 to build the CyberCom force has raised concerns about the feasibility of scaling up the workforce so quickly.[14] In 2012, General Alexander (Ret.) reported, "At present we are critically short of the skills and the

---

[12]   Alexander, 2013a. This was also reported in our expert interviews.

[13]   Defense Science Board, 2013.

[14]   Starks, 2013; Defense Science Board, 2013; Serbu, 2012.

skilled people we as a Command and a nation require to manage our networks and protect U.S. interests in cyberspace."[15] The services have been making progress toward meeting new demand, yet 2013 reports suggest than an additional 3,700 cyber warriors are needed, so training will need to continue at accelerated levels and could potentially be expanded to meet these needs.[16] In addition, the service-specific needs for cyber expertise are growing, so it is likely that the demand for cyber warriors for these missions will continue to increase as well.

The lack of a common standard for determining which positions are included in the cyber warrior workforce makes it challenging to assess workforce need. Cyber workforce reports therefore look at different populations, and reported levels of demand for cyber warriors vary by service and the source in which they were reported. For example, the 24th Air Force has identified a need for 1,000 additional new hires for cyber defense—mostly civilian—beginning in 2014, and the Army also plans to add an additional 1,000 individuals to its cyber workforce.[17] In the 2011 Personnel Report, DoD reported that the Army needed additional capacity in Intelligence and Security Command, and the Marine Corps acknowledged needs for cyber planners, source analysts, and information assurance technical managers.[18] In addition, the Joint Staffs, five of the combatant commands, and six defense agencies noted a need for additional cyber personnel. A 2011 GAO report cites common reports of a need for cyber planners and cyber-focused intelligence officials by the combatant commands.[19] These needs are likely to have changed somewhat since the series of reports that were released in 2011. For example, a 2013 report by the Defense Science

---

[15] Alexander, 2012.

[16] Fryer-Biggs, 2013.

[17] Magnuson, 2013; Joe Gould, "Be an Army Hacker: This Top Secret Cyber Unit Wants You," *Army Times*, April 8, 2013.

[18] Department of Defense, 2011b.

[19] GAO, 2011.

Board acknowledges a need to focus on developing offensive cyber warriors, given the increasing role of offensive cyber operations.[20]

The need to rapidly scale up certain cyber warfare capabilities and the substantial time required to screen and train these cyber warriors have driven concerns about the ability to meet workforce needs, at least in the short term. However, there is little quantitative evidence to compare the available supply of cyber warriors to demand, particularly given the challenges in defining the workforce. Government agencies must compete with private industry for cyber warriors, as private companies are also facing increased demand for individuals in cyber security. Given that private entities are often able to pay higher salaries, there may be challenges in recruiting a sufficient number of cyber warriors to military service and retaining them. However, further analysis is still needed to determine whether a real and persistent shortage exists among the cyber warrior workforce. Regardless of whether there is a shortage of cyber warriors in DoD, the substantial investments DoD will make to meet workforce needs suggest that it will be important to ensure that the approaches to training are as effective and efficient as possible.

Existing Training for Cyber Warriors

To support rapid growth in the cyber warrior workforce, there is a range of training options in place for the military and civilian workforces. Rather than providing an exhaustive list of the training options, we highlight some of the main opportunities described by our cyber experts and cyber military resources.

Central/Joint Training Opportunities

The centralized or joint training opportunity that was most commonly discussed by the experts and the literature was the Joint Cyber Analysis Course (JCAC). JCAC is a six-month course provided at the Center for Information Dominance, located at the Navy's Correy Station base in Pensacola, Florida. The course is intended to train individuals to meet

---

[20] Defense Science Board, 2013.

a wide range of cyber missions. While initially a Navy course, it is now used for cyber warrior training across all of the services. According to the experts we interviewed, the National Security Agency (NSA) is closely involved in driving the content of the training to ensure that it meets joint defense needs in cyber warfare capabilities. After individuals complete JCAC, a portion of the trainees with the highest potential to become cyber warriors are identified to receive additional training in the NSA environment.

The course is viewed as one of the more advanced training courses available to cyber warriors, and it is generally reserved for the individuals who show the greatest promise. The services use various methods to identify individuals to be sent to JCAC. For example, according to one expert, the Air Force reserves this training for enlisted individuals who have been retrained to highly specialized cyber career fields after being screened according to performance and cyber aptitude. Most individuals do not enter these career fields until at least four to six years into military service. After spending 24 weeks in an intermediate service-specific training course, cyber warriors are sent to JCAC and additional on-the-job training in the NSA environment. Between the coursework and the on-the-job component, this advanced training requires a full year. To ensure that this investment in training pays off, the Air Force requires participants to sign an additional three-year service commitment.

To support the development of joint training and coordinate the management of cyber workforces across the services, DoD is engaged in efforts to define job roles, identify KSAs needed for these job roles, and develop a clear link to the training that is required to provide these skills.[21] The operational training framework will be organized around 42 specific roles in the DoD workforce. According to one article, the first focus is on members of the defense workforce who are specifically tasked with computer network defense.[22] However, the cyber experts we interviewed argued that precise job descriptions and associated skills are not as easily developed for cyber warriors, where the job that

---

[21] Serbu, 2012.

[22] Serbu, 2012.

is being performed is more of an art than a technical skill set. They report that CyberCom is making headway on this effort, and there remains hope that the certification and guidance on training needs will be expanded to the more highly specialized cyber warrior positions as these job roles become more familiar and a set of skills associated with success can be identified.

Service-Specific Training

There is a range of efforts taking place within the services to train cyber warriors for service-specific operations and joint missions. For example, the U.S. Air Force has a number of training courses to support military personnel involved in offensive and defensive operations. Among the enlisted, individuals are brought into traditional career fields, which allows for an opportunity to prescreen individuals to determine whether they are qualified for cyber operations. After some time in the service, individuals who show promise are provided with undergraduate cyber training and are retrained to join the core cyber operations team (1B4s). In return for an additional service commitment, these individuals who have reached more advanced levels of proficiency have the opportunity to complete Intermediate Network Warfare Training, which is a 24-week course in cyber operations. After this intermediate training, some of the most talented individuals are sent on to the joint training through JCAC. The Air Force also has courses designed for officers to improve the leadership of cyber operations, such as their Cyber 200 course for captains and their Cyber 300 course for majors.

The Navy, Marine Corps, and Army also provide a range of courses in cyber operations. A search of the Army course catalogue identifies 23 different cyber courses at National Cryptologic School, the Signal School, and the Joint Warfighter Center. However, it is unclear how many of these courses focus on training for cyber warriors, as opposed to individuals working in information assurance and cyber-related positions. Cyber warriors are also developed through on-the-job training, as soldiers are put through a series of developmental assignments that can take three to five years.[23] In the Navy, JCAC (described above) continues to be used heavily in training cyber warriors. In addition, individuals can enroll in graduate programs at the Naval Postgraduate School and take other courses at Navy installations.

Colleges and Centers of Academic Excellence

The Centers of Academic Excellence (CAEs) were established in 1999 to provide cyber education in information assurance. The number of CAEs has expanded rapidly, from just seven in 1999 to 117 in 2011.[24] In 2010, an additional set of two-year colleges was identified for the CAE two-year programs. However, until recently, these CAEs focused exclusively on information assurance and did not have the capability to train highly specialized cyber warriors. In 2012, the NSA and Department of Homeland Security announced a new set of CAEs for cyber operations.[25] At the time of this report, there were four programs: Dakota State University in South Dakota, the Naval Postgraduate School in California, Northeastern University in Massachusetts, and the University of Tulsa in Oklahoma.

According to the NSA website, the CAE—Cyber Operations program is intended to be a deeply technical, interdisciplinary program firmly grounded in the computer science and computer and/ or electrical engineering disciplines, with extensive opportunities for hands-on applications via labs and exercises. According to an expert from a CAE, approximately two-thirds of the students in cyber programs are military, while the rest are civilian. According to our expert interviews, many of these students are supported through DoD and other federal funding programs, such as Scholarship for Service and the Information Assurance Scholarship Program. These programs typically require a federal service commitment to receive education funding. While these cyber CAEs are quickly being scaled up to meet the need for additional cyber warriors, our interviews suggest that there is

---

[23] Joe Gould, "Army Ramps Up Cybersecurity Skills Training," *Army Times*, November 19, 2012.

[24] DoD, 2011b.

[25] NSA, "List of Centers of Academic Excellence for Cyber Operations," 2014.

room for improvement. According to one expert who is involved with this training, the CAEs are doing a good job of producing high-quality information assurance experts, but they have so far been less successful in producing cyber warriors—individuals who engage in offensive and defensive cyber operations.

The military academies have also been building up their capacity to provide more advanced education opportunities around cyber warfare. In 2012–2013, both the U.S. Naval Academy and the U.S. Air Force Academy offered majors in cyber operations for the first time.[26] A new Cyber Research Center was developed at the U.S. Military Academy, though the school has yet to develop a major in cyber operations.

Competitions and Outreach

DoD and the federal agencies have developed a range of competitions and outreach strategies to provide real-life training opportunities and build the pipeline of potential cyber warriors. Cyber Flag exercises at Nellis Air Force Base bring together more than 300 DoD cyber warriors to engage in joint cyber challenges.[27] Every year NSA conducts the Cyber Defense Exercise, which engages students from the military academies to fight hackers who attempt to invade test networks.[28] Hacking competitions were also developed for high school cyber teams, including the Digital Forensic Challenge and CyberPatriot. The National Defense University iCollege also conducts a range of outreach activities. According to the cyber experts interviewed for this study, these competitions are effective in screening and building the profile of the cyber community. However, these competitions do not necessarily prioritize training and development, so improvements, such as more-realistic scenarios, could be made to ensure that they are building capacity.

---

[26] Brian Witte and Dan Elliot, "Air Force Academy Training Cadets for Cyberwarfare," *Standard-Examiner*, April 26, 2013; Steve Blank, "Flying High: Why the Military Is Taking Cyber Warfare Seriously," *Forbes*, April 29, 2013.

[27] See U.S. Army Cyber Command, "U.S. Cyber Command Conducts Tactical Cyber Exercise," *Sound Off!*, undated.

[28] DoD, 2011b.

Industry

According to several of our experts, many of the training materials and approaches that are used by the military were initially drawn from industry. Contractors play a substantial role in delivering training as well. One of the key initiatives in DoD's cyber strategy is to build partnerships with the business community, and these partnerships can be used to share strategies for training elite cyber warriors.[29] However, to the degree that DoD cyber operations are really at the "cutting edge" of cyber warfare—and in many cases involve actions that may be illegal in the civilian world—the lessons that can be drawn from industry may be limited. In particular, industry will have substantial experience with defensive operations but may have little to offer in training approaches for offensive operations.

Training as Part of a Larger Workforce Management Strategy

While it is beyond the scope of this study to describe and address all of the potential issues with workforce management, to the degree that these impact a training strategy, they are important to consider. An effective and efficient training strategy for cyber warriors will need to take into consideration all aspects of the pipeline for cyber warriors, from recruiting and hiring to placement to retention. For example, the experts we interviewed emphasized that the level of entering ability has a substantial impact on what can be taught and the level of resources that will be needed to bring individuals to required levels of expertise. This suggests that efforts to build a strong pipeline have direct implications for the approach that may be taken to training. The reliance on enlisted military as cyber warriors makes the consideration of the entire pipeline particularly important: Because these individuals typically enter with little training, the military is wholly responsible for developing these individuals into cyber warriors. It can take years for individuals to be

---

[29] DoD, 2011a.

screened and trained, and so planning must anticipate future needs to ensure sufficient time to recruit and/or train cyber warriors.

There are also concerns about retaining and managing the workforce. The extensive training required for cyber warriors is likely to be costly, so the return on this investment is an important consideration. Several of our interviewees reported that highly trained cyber warriors are often mismanaged upon completing training, ending up in positions that do not require expertise in cyber warfare, as happens with those in other professions as well. According to our interviewees and the literature, there is a concern that competition for highly qualified cyber warriors from industry and other federal agencies, with wages and advancement opportunities that exceed those available in the military, may draw the most highly qualified cyber warriors away from DoD.[30] On the other hand, several experts we interviewed and the literature suggest that the opportunity to be a part of the most cutting-edge cyber warfare often outweighs monetary benefits and helps to support DoD recruitment and hiring. A specialized career path was mentioned throughout the literature and our interviews as an important way of increasing retention and improving workforce management. Additional research is needed to understand whether cyber warriors face the same challenges with retention that have been observed with highly trained experts in other fields.

The Future of Cyber Warfare

The cyber field is rapidly evolving, and cyber training needs are likely to be an area of intense DoD focus for several decades to come. DoD faces an expanding and varied set of threats in the cyber world that may increase the scope of missions that national forces face.[31] As the mission expands, training will need to be enhanced. As the workforce needs change, the training strategy must account for these changes and make adjustments quickly. According to the Defense Science Board,

---

[30] Serbu, 2012; U.S. Navy, 2013.

[31] Clapper, 2013; Defense Science Board, 2013.

"DoD needs to develop training programs with evolving content that reflects the changing threat, increases individual knowledge, and continually reinforces policy."[32]

In addition to growth in offensive cyber warfare efforts, a number of trends may impact the cyber workforce and defense training needs. One substantial change that may impact cyber training is the transition to the Joint Information Environment (JIE). DoD is currently working to bring all of the services under a single cloud environment to improve the ability to monitor activities taking place within DoD's computing systems and to reduce the need to protect multiple environments.[33] According to one expert, the ability to work in this new environment will place a substantial training burden on DoD, as individuals must be trained in both the old and new environments as the transition is made. In the area of offensive operations, newly developed weapon systems will likely require new training content and potentially shape training delivery. Efficiency will also be important in an increasingly constrained budget environment. A successful training strategy will not only identify the best ways to train cyber warriors, but will also consider ways of doing this that minimize the use of resources.

We next turn to a description of defense language training and highlight the areas in which the current system of training is working and where it is challenged, in order to draw messages that may inform planning and policymaking for cyber training.

---

[32] Defense Science Board, 2013.

[33] General Keith B. Alexander (Ret.), Commander of United States Cyber Command, "Cybersecurity: Preparing for and Responding to an Enduring Threat," Statement to the Senate Committee on Appropriations, June 12, 2013b.

CHAPTER THREE

Overview of Defense Language Training, Successes, and Challenges

Because (1) Americans are most commonly monolingual English speakers,[1] (2) the U.S. education system provides limited opportunities for students to learn other languages in comparison to those offered in multilingual countries,[2] and (3) security concerns may restrict the eligibility of foreign-born personnel who are native speakers of critically needed languages, U.S. defense agencies provide substantial amounts of training to meet the need for language-skilled personnel. In this chapter, we provide a broad overview of U.S defense language training and discuss insights from interviews and the literature about successes and challenges in the field.

The Delivery of Language Training

Language Training Institutes and Programs

Under current conditions, most military personnel who will become language specialists must be trained from zero or from a very low skill level to become linguists or cryptologists. The Defense Language Institute Foreign Language Center (DLIFLC), established by the

---

[1] C. Ryan, *Language Use in the United States: 2011*, U.S. Census, 2013; F. Grosjean, "Bilingualism's Best-Kept Secret: How Extensive It Is," *Psychology Today*, 2010.

[2] N. C. Rhodes and I. Pufahl, *Foreign Language Teaching in U.S. Schools: Results of a National Survey*, Center for Applied Linguistics, 2009; D. Skorton and G. Altschuler. "America's Foreign-Language Deficit," *Forbes*, August 27, 2012.

U.S. Army in the 1940s just before the United States entered World
War II, is a primary mechanism for training military personnel in languages of importance to national security. Although it is under the
control of the U.S. Army Training and Doctrine Command, it serves
as a joint institute, training students from the Army, Navy, Air Force,
Marine Corps, and other U.S. government agencies. The majority of
its students are enlisted personnel who attend the school to be trained
from zero to intermediate and advanced levels of proficiency quickly.
It teaches more than 20 different languages and can accommodate
approximately 4,200 students.[3] It provides what experts consistently
described as "global language and culture instruction" and is a common
entry point to language training for enlisted military personnel. After
DLIFLC, individuals may be sent for further, more specialized or more
advanced training elsewhere, such as National Cryptologic School or
a program at a military base, such as Fort Meade, where they receive
training that may take them from intermediate to advanced or train
them for specific duties using the target language.

A number of other language training programs exist, including those offered through the National Cryptologic School, the Foreign Service Institute (FSI), and CIA University, among others—with
each designed to train students for specific purposes. For example, the
Foreign Service Institute School of Language Studies[4] trains officers
and support personnel of the U.S. foreign affairs community, including diplomats and others who work in foreign affairs. The National
Cryptologic School trains cryptologists, many of whom work in the
intersection between language and cyber on responsibilities including signals intelligence, information assurance, and computer network
operations. It trains individuals with higher skill levels and focuses on
mission-related materials. CIA University offers language training to
intelligence analysts in the Central Intelligence Agency. In addition to
those channels, a number of military agencies also provide substantial
language and culture training. For example, U.S. Special Operations
Command and the U.S. Air Force, Navy, and Marine Corps all provide

---

[3] Defense Language Institute Foreign Language Center General Catalog, 2011–2012.

[4] U.S. Department of State, "Foreign Service Institute," undated.

specialized, mission-specific language training to selected personnel. Every military organization with language-skilled professionals is also required to have a Command Language Program, which is responsible for helping personnel maintain or enhance existing language skills.[5]

Colleges and Universities

Language programs in postsecondary institutions also play an important role in language training. For example, the immersion programs at Middlebury College in Vermont and the intensive language programs at Monterey Institute for International Studies in California offer extensive language instruction. In some cases, military officers and government personnel may be sent to a college- or university-based language program for intensive study.

In addition, the DoD National Security Education Program and the Defense Language Office (merged in 2012 into the Defense Language and National Security Education Office) have undertaken a number of initiatives to partner with universities to develop expertise in critical languages, cultures, and regions with strategic importance to U.S. interests.

The first of these, the Language Flagship Program, was established in 2002 with the goal of establishing a new way for the U.S. education system to produce advanced speakers of languages critical to U.S. national security.[6] It began by funding a small number of U.S. universities to establish innovative advanced language education programs in Korean, Arabic, Chinese, and Russian and educate students to reach an advanced level of proficiency that would enable them to function as professionals in U.S. government jobs in the target languages. As of 2013, there are 26 university-based Flagship Centers, providing instruction in Arabic, Chinese, Hindi-Urdu, Korean, Persian, Portuguese, Russian, Swahili, and Turkish.[7] Graduates of university-level Flagship programs are expected to serve in government agencies upon

---

[5]   Defense Language Institute Foreign Language Center, "Command Language Program Support," undated.

[6]   Language Flagship, home page, 2013.

[7]   Language Flagship, "The Flagship History," 2012.

completing their programs. The Flagship initiative also includes funding for K–12 education to extend the model to the early years of students' education and build the pipeline of second-language–proficient individuals in the U.S. workforce.

In 2007, DoD launched Project GO,[8] an initiative designed to improve the language skills, regional expertise, and intercultural communication skills of future U.S. military officers. As of 2013, the program provides institutional grants to 22 U.S. universities, including five of the six senior military colleges. The grants fund the building of university capabilities in critical languages—including Arabic, Chinese, Hausa, Hindi-Urdu, Persian, Pashto, Russian, Swahili, Uzbek, and Wolof—and provide scholarships to Reserve Officer Training Corps students for study of those languages in the United States and overseas.

In 2012, the National Security Education Program funded a new initiative, the Language Training Centers, to develop expertise in critical languages, cultures, and regions for DoD personnel. The first funding awards went to five universities: California State University, Long Beach; North Carolina State University; North Georgia College and State University; San Diego State University; and the University of Montana. The vision is that the Language Training Centers will help meet DoD total force language training needs.[9]

Commercial and Contract Language Training Providers

In addition to the U.S. government and military training schools and programs and the university partnerships, a good deal of language training takes place through outside providers. The services and other government agencies commonly outsource basic language training to commercial providers, such as Berlitz and Inlingua, or to small business language training organizations. Many of these language contractors work exclusively for DoD, and interviewees described them as highly responsive to government's needs. They provide a variety of

---

8   Project GO, "Program Overview," 2013.

9   National Security Education Program, "Language Training Centers," 2013.

services, including group instruction, distance learning, and one-on-one tutoring.

Shared Definitions and Metrics

Our discussion of the cyber warrior population and the larger cyber workforce acknowledged a need for a better-defined workforce and greater coordination of training efforts. The defense language community has dealt with some of these challenges and may offer lessons to the cyber field for forming and using definitions and metrics across the field. In this section, we describe a few of the established tools, standards, and definitions that contribute to shared understanding across the field and improved ability to develop the workforce.

Screening

Two screening tests play critical roles in the defense language training infrastructure. Although DLIFLC trains students from a variety of backgrounds, the vast majority are enlisted personnel from the services who enter with little or no knowledge of the language they are assigned to learn. Candidate screening takes place primarily by way of the Defense Language Aptitude Battery (DLAB), a test designed to identify those who will be successful in learning a new language. DLAB scores help determine whether an individual is sent for language training and in what language he or she will be trained. For those with existing language skills, the Defense Language Placement Test (DLPT) is used to assess one's current level of proficiency and may be used to determine job assignments, bonus pay eligibility, or placement in further training. The services also use the Armed Services Vocational Aptitude Battery (ASVAB),[10] which measures multiple aptitudes, to select individuals to attend language training.

---

[10] ASVAB, home page, undated.

Skill Descriptions

Defense language training benefits from a common set of metrics for language proficiency. The Interagency Language Roundtable Scale[11] describes six levels of language skills in the four domains of listening, reading, speaking, and writing. Its development began in the 1950s after a government commission highlighted the need for a measurement system that was objective, applicable to all languages and all jobs, and unrelated to any particular language curriculum.[12] It has continually evolved over the years and remains a common reference for language training and assessment for the U.S. government. Outside of government, another scale, developed by the American Council on the Teaching of Foreign Languages, an association of language educators and other professionals, is commonly used, and there is a widely accepted crosswalk between the two scales.

Categories of Difficulty

Language training benefits further from established categories of difficulty that correspond to the amount of time and effort needed for a native speaker of English to learn specific languages. The Defense Language Institute (DLI) categorizes languages into levels of difficulty based on the number of weeks of intensive instruction typically required for an adult native speaker of English to reach a given level of proficiency.[13] For example, Spanish and Portuguese, which take less time to learn, are in Category 1, while Chinese and Arabic, which are among the most difficult to learn, are in Category 4. FSI has developed a similar categorization, dividing languages into three categories of difficulty.[14]

---

[11]   Interagency Language Roundtable, "Descriptions of Proficiency Levels," undated[b].

[12]   Interagency Language Roundtable, "An Overview of the History of the ILR Language Proficiency Skill Level Descriptions and Scale by Dr. Martha Herzog," undated[a].

[13]   Defense Language Institute Foreign Language Center General Catalog, 2011–2012.

[14]   Foreign Service Institute, *Language Continuum*, Arlington, Va.: U.S. Department of State, 2004.

Successes in Language Training

Interviewees highlighted a number of areas in which they view the current system of language training as working well.

Training to Specific Needs

When asked about elements in the field of defense language training that are working well, a number of interviewees expressed the view that the existing government training institutes and programs do well at training to specific needs. For example, DLIFLC was described as effective for providing global language and culture training in a highly focused environment, free of distractions, in an unclassified setting. Interviewees noted its greater emphasis on receptive skills, such as listening and reading, while other providers, such as FSI, focus more on speaking and interacting. Moreover, language training provided through Special Operations Command differs in other ways, such as training to lower skill levels, depending on the mission. Other schools, such as the National Cryptologic School and CIA University, have the infrastructure to provide training in a cleared environment if needed. Interviewees commented that the various training programs meet a wide variety of different needs.

Screening

Interviewees pointed to the screening mechanisms in place, specifically the DLAB, as assets that facilitated training. Being able to screen candidates and select those with the most promise makes training more efficient by reducing attrition, thus reducing wasted resources. While the existence of the DLAB was widely acknowledged as an asset, some experts commented about the need to strengthen it and other aptitude assessment tools to improve screening. One interviewee described substantial efforts to revise the DLAB, but the changes had not been fully implemented at the time of this study.

Shared Definitions and Metrics

The Interagency Language Roundtable scale and skill-level descriptions provide common reference points across all language training efforts.

Across our interviews of language experts, individuals were able to refer to specific levels of proficiency on a common scale. For example, a 2+/2+/2 in Arabic, representing intermediate proficiency in listening/reading/speaking, refers to the same level of skill whether the individual is in the Air Force, Army, Navy, or Marine Corps or at NSA, CIA, or some other agency. Scales and metrics like this give all stakeholders a common understanding of the goals of training. These measures enable those providing training, measuring skills, and employing those who possess the skills to have a shared understanding of training goals and outcomes.

Meeting Diverse Needs of Many Stakeholders

Although interviewees acknowledged shortcomings in the system, the picture that emerged when considering the numerous channels for language training—which include central or joint resources, service- and agency-specific training schools and programs, and universities and commercial providers, as well a common set of standards and metrics—is a system that accommodates a wide range of needs and is able to respond to emerging demands for specific languages. It encompasses a range of institutions—such as DLIFLC, National Cryptologic School, FSI, and CIA University—and the vast number of programs provided by the services, universities, and commercial providers, each targeted to different populations and needs. The experts we interviewed described the existing system as being able to provide training at basic through advanced levels and tailored to a variety of missions.

Access to a Joint Training Resource

While views were mixed, some experts commented that the existence of an established joint training resource, such as DLIFLC, offered advantages because it provided a single source for basic, global language and culture training and relieved individual agencies from having to duplicate one another's efforts. One expert pointed out that it also provides a locus for a "critical mass" of training expertise in the field. Others expressed the view that a central institute for defense language was better able to focus on the needs of defense and national security than most universities would be, but they acknowledged that cyber could differ substantially because of the much larger universe of options available in that field of expertise. For example, cyber expertise comprises a large range of subspecializations and knowledge in the field evolves quickly, in contrast to language, in which change is not as rapid or potentially widespread.

Challenges in Language Training

Limited Pipeline of Language-Skilled Personnel

The limited pipeline of language-skilled personnel was a recurring theme in the interviews. Several of the experts interviewed commented that the U.S. education system does not produce enough individuals with language expertise. They expressed the view that beginning language training at age 18, when individuals are past the optimal age for second-language learning, is too late and thus not the best approach. Research supports these assertions.[15] A number of experts expressed strong views that language education should start earlier, in K–12 education, similar to the numerous initiatives currently in place with science, technology, engineering, and mathematics (STEM) education.

A stronger pipeline of language-skilled individuals would bring larger numbers of more prepared students to the military and government service. It would also ease pressure on institutions that are tasked with training adult students with little to no second-language capabilities. Furthermore, it would reduce the overall training needs and make training more efficient because students who already know a second language tend to learn additional languages more quickly.[16]

In addition to building skills among enlisted individuals before entering the military to build the pipeline, DoD could also consider altering the mix of the language workforce—for example, by employ-

---

[15] Robert M. DeKeyser, "The Robustness of Critical Period Effects in Second Language Acquisition," *Studies in Second Language Acquisition*, Vol. 22, 2000, pp. 499–533.

[16] W. P. Rivers and E. M. Golonka, "Third Language Acquisition Theory and Practice," in M. Long and C. Doughty, eds., *The Handbook of Language Teaching*, New York: Wiley-Blackwell, 2009.

ing more civilians—to reduce the training burden. Furthermore, if restrictions on eligibility were reduced, the pipeline could come to include a greater number of native speakers of other languages. Such changes could expand the number of eligible individuals who already have skills in critical languages. However, as noted, recruiting policies would need to be revised.

Time Required to Train to High Levels of Proficiency

As most students enter defense language training with no second-language skills, training providers face the substantial challenge of developing their skills quickly. Some experts expressed the view that existing programs, including DLIFLC, take too long. However, they acknowledged that the problem is not necessarily the fault of the institutions, and it may be related to resources, as well as the aptitude and motivation of the students.

Need to Better Share Resources

Some experts commented that the existing institutions and language training programs do a weak job sharing resources and therefore fail to leverage the expertise of other organizations doing similar work. As a result, they may end up duplicating one another's efforts in terms of developing training materials. One of the interviewees acknowledged that this could be due to the fast pace and time constraints associated with developing and implementing training programs.

Need to Improve Most University-Based Language Training

Interviewees commented on the challenges of relying on universities for training. With the exception of the Flagship universities and a select few others, they stated that most university language programs are not oriented toward practical usage or proficiency goals, and many are taught by inexperienced instructors, such as graduate students. In addition, some interviewees commented that universities tend to be less responsive than other providers, and university faculty are generally unfamiliar with the government and military mission.

Although interviewees expressed positive views of the DoD-funded Flagship programs, some noted that the programs have faced difficulties placing graduates into government jobs because appropriate job openings did not exist at the time graduates were applying.

High Cost

A number of experts commented on the high cost of language training, with estimates well into six figures for a single student starting from zero. Just to acquire a basic foundation in a second language requires months, and it commonly requires several years to build skills to advanced proficiency.[17] These expenses could be reduced if more individuals entered military service with second-language skills or if attrition from training programs could be reduced. Coupled with retention challenges (which we discuss next), the high cost of language training results in a limited return on investment.

Retention Challenges

A recurring theme in the interviews was the challenge of retaining personnel after they have been trained, which is also a workforce management issue. The government may invest hundreds of thousands of dollars in training an individual, not only initially, but also throughout his or her career; however, market forces may draw her or him away from military service, or the typical military career progression may move him or her onto other jobs that do not require language skills. In addition, individuals may view military service as a step in one's professional development, rather than a long-term career choice. Some, but not all, training opportunities are offered with corresponding service commitments. A number of the experts we interviewed suggested the possibility of more service commitments for training to aid retention. One also recommended designing career paths that motivate people to stay by offering individuals increasing responsibility aligned with their interests.

---

[17] Note that research is under way to identify ways to accelerate language learning; for example, E. Hussey and J. Novick, "The Benefits of Executive Control Training and the Implications for Language Processing," *Frontiers in Psychology*, Vol. 3, 2012; and J. Novick, E. Hussey, S. Teubner-Rhodes, J. Harbison, and M. Bunting. "Clearing the Garden-Path: Improving Sentence Processing Through Cognitive Control Training," *Language and Cognitive Processes*, 2013.

Competing Management Priorities

As mentioned earlier, DLIFLC, which serves as a joint training institute for many agencies, originated as an Army training center, and it remains under the control of the Army Training and Doctrine Command. As a result, when competing priorities exist, the Army's prevail over those of other services and agencies. One expert suggested that it might be better placed under the control of the NSA, rather than with one of the services. Another expert, who held similar views, commented that it might be better managed as a DoD activity, rather than remaining within a military service.

Summary

In this chapter, we gave a brief overview of defense language training. We described the ways in which defense language training is delivered—through government and service-related institutes and programs, universities, and commercial providers. We also described the shared definitions and metrics that the field uses, including aptitude and placement tests, skill-level descriptions, and categories of difficulty that allow practitioners in the field to make decisions based on established standards. We then highlighted the areas that experts described as working well: They considered the field effective in its ability to train to specific needs, use shared definitions and metrics, meet diverse needs, and access a joint training resource. The experts identified a number of challenges as well, including the limited pipeline of eligible, skilled personnel; the length of time required to reach high levels of proficiency; cost; retention; and management. In the next chapter, we explain how these topics fit into a framework that can inform cyber training.

CHAPTER FOUR

Key Considerations for Developing an Effective and Efficient Training Strategy for Cyber Warriors

The previous chapters document the range of training activities that are taking place in both the cyber and language fields. In Chapter Three, we described some of the things that have been particularly successful in language training, as well as other areas in which there are challenges.

Our interviews with experts across both fields and our review of the literature pointed to a set of common issues that were highlighted as important to consider in developing a training strategy for both language and cyber. Realizing that these considerations can be applied to developing training across many fields and workforces of different levels of expertise, we organized these key issues into a framework for developing a training strategy (Figure 4.1). The framework centers on four key questions:

- What will the training look like?
- Who is being trained?
- What resources are needed to support the training?
- How will the training fit into overall workforce management?

In this chapter, we illustrate the importance of these issues through evidence from our interviews and the literature. We describe the experiences of the cyber warrior community in addressing these issues and identify parallels in the language community.

Figure 4.1
Key Considerations for an Effective and Efficient Training Strategy

RAND *RR476-4.1*

Common Definitions and Standards

Before it is possible to address the four questions of focus, it is critical to establish a clear common language to discuss needs for cyber capabilities and the workforce that meets these needs. We therefore consider this component—common definitions and standards—central to the training decisionmaking framework. The cyber literature and discussions with cyber experts suggest that there is still substantial work to be done in defining which occupations and activities fall under the cyber workforce and the various subcomponents of the cyber workforce, like cyber warriors. Language, on the other hand, has been successful in defining the capabilities needed and subsequently tracking these capabilities across the workforce, and our language experts reported that this common understanding of the workforce and its needs have been helpful in supporting the training strategy.

A lack of clarity in cyber about what capabilities are needed in the workforce and how existing resources are being used to meet these needs limits the possibilities for ensuring that training is effective and efficient, because the training cannot be closely tailored to workforce needs, and it will be difficult to track the outcomes of various approaches to evaluate and refine their effectiveness and efficiency. In addition to a definition of the work that is being done under cyber and a description of the current workforce that is operating in cyber roles, experts expressed a need for standards, including a common certification system and metrics to track and more effectively manage the cyber workforce. This may require a significant departure from the current system, which focuses on relatively imprecise categories of skills and functions and does not capture the more specific skill sets that are needed to manage highly skilled populations.

Several experts acknowledged that a common certification system and other metrics to track skill levels may be useful for the information assurance community, but not as useful for the individuals at the highest levels of expertise, because it is difficult to assess the skills of these individuals in a systematic way. In addition, while proficiency in language is a somewhat stable target, proficiency in cyber warfare is a rapidly moving target, making it more difficult to develop and track meaningful metrics. Even after the capabilities necessary for cyber warfare are defined, there is still a need to understand the workforce and account for the training and management of individuals in the workforce. Metrics to define the makeup of the workforce, account for the training individuals have received, and understand movement throughout careers would be valuable at all levels of cyber expertise by allowing for assessment of whether predetermined capabilities are being met. As CyberCom works to establish a better means of identifying and classifying cyber warrior capabilities and the associated workforce, it may be useful to draw from the experiences of the language community in describing the language workforce.

What Will the Training Look Like?

Before assessing the population that makes up the existing cyber warrior workforce and pipeline, it is important to identify what capabilities are needed for cyber warfare and what training will best serve these needs. Clearly outlining workforce capability needs will help to determine who is needed to achieve these capabilities, and by comparing these needs to the existing workforce, gaps in KSAs can be identified. This will help to ensure that the content and delivery of the training is carefully tailored to fill these identified skill gaps, which will maximize the effectiveness and efficiency of the training. This section describes three considerations that were mentioned by the literature and experts in the language and cyber fields as critical to driving training content: mission, platform (e.g., computing environments, network structure), and job roles and their associated KSAs. We also discuss the delivery of training and its importance in effectively developing highly specialized skill sets like cyber and language.

Mission

Whether the field is language or cyber, mission plays a key role in determining the content of training, as well as having important implications for the organization and delivery of training. The importance of mission-focused training was one of the most commonly discussed issues among experts in both fields, with nine of the experts interviewed arguing that mission focus and/or "training with context" is critical in ensuring that the training is effective and efficient in preparing individuals for their specific job needs. According to experts in the language field, it is imperative that linguists receive mission-based training to ensure that they are able to operationalize their skills in a real-world environment. Defense missions require a unique set of skills from linguists, and many of these are best developed through training that is structured around mission-specific activities. Cyber experts cited a similar need for mission focus in the training provided to cyber warriors.

At least nine of the experts across language and cyber argued that to the degree the mission is common across a workforce, it is useful to have common training. If cyber warriors are focused on unique service-specific missions, then the services will have the deepest knowledge of these mission needs and are likely to have an advantage in quickly training up cyber warriors to meet this need. To the degree that national or joint missions will play a larger role in cyber operations relative to service-specific missions, central coordination of training may be important, as it will help to avoid duplication and allow for better coordination as the warriors work side by side on these cyber missions. This standardization can occur through a central institute or could be provided by the services and coordinated by a central body.

From the language field, end users of DLI graduates, such as NSA, have been closely involved in advising DLI on mission needs—and, according to some of our interviewees, DLI has been responsive in meeting those needs for training up to a certain level of skill. Beyond that level, NSA provides its own training through the National Cryptologic School. This training is meant to train individuals to reach higher levels of language proficiency and master mission-based content. One expert in our interviews commented that the location of DLI under Army Training and Doctrine Command sometimes leads to an uneven focus on Army needs relative to other services and agencies.

According to three of the experts from cyber, there is some tension between service needs and CyberCom needs, and there is a concern that the central needs would take priority if training were centralized. A March 2013 speech by General Alexander (Ret.) asserted that the CyberCom mission teams will serve both the mission needs of the services and the mission needs of CyberCom, but it is unclear to those in the services how well these missions will coincide.[1] Yet, several experts noted that these missions are often quite different and require distinctly different skill sets, and there is a concern that workforce needs for national missions and intelligence missions will dominate training content, particularly given the close relationship between NSA and cyber. For example, one Air Force expert argued that the JCAC course provides a number of advanced intelligence skills that are extremely valuable for cyber warriors working in intelligence but are not needed

---

[1]   Alexander, 2013a.

for most service-specific operations. Rather than training all individuals to the highest level in the full range of capabilities needed for national missions, intelligence operations, and service-specific activities, the Air Force expert argued that a segmented approach could more efficiently train up the highly skilled cyber warrior workforce by providing a range of training options (both central and service-specific) that prepare individuals for different types of missions.

The experts we interviewed strongly believed that advanced training should be mission-based, and they pointed to universities' lack of contextual knowledge and understanding of the mission to be one of the major drawbacks of using universities for advanced education and training for both the language and cyber fields. In the language field, universities often focus on the contexts of literature, travel, or business to drive the design of coursework. Once the individuals trained in universities join the military or civilian DoD workforces, they must be provided with an additional series of trainings to understand how to apply their skills to military missions. The Flagship universities and CAEs are one method of developing stronger partnerships with DoD to ensure that individuals are being provided with the capabilities required for defense missions. One expert suggested that more-regular rotations of military experts through the universities might help to create even stronger ties with mission needs, as the lack of people in the schools with a real knowledge of military issues limits the education these students receive.

Platform

The systems that will be used to conduct military operations are also important in determining the content of training and the strategy for delivering training. In some ways, this is an issue that is unique to cyber, but it can be analogous to learning different languages, as both computer systems/platforms and languages act as "tools" to support operations. On the defensive side, the services currently work in different network environments, so training must focus on preparing cyber warriors to operate in the environment used by their service. However, DoD is in the process of transitioning to JIE, a common DoD network. When all of the services are working in a common environment, there will be more overlap in what cyber experts need to learn, and likely a greater role in cyber training. In the short term, however, one expert noted that the migration to a joint environment will lead to an increase in training needs, as many in the cyber warrior workforce will need to know how to work on the old service-specific systems as well as the new system.

According to the experts, much of the work is currently being carried out on centralized computer systems. Given that, it may make sense to have training centralized and focused on the intricacies of that particular environment. However, according to one expert, exclusive focus on that environment for offensive warfare would miss a number of opportunities to conduct smaller-scale offensive operations with less sophisticated computer systems. According to this expert, "Many of the people we are most concerned about attacking us are working on machines that cost less than $1,000." If the services were able to employ their best cyber warriors on simpler computer systems in environments with lower levels of security, the expert argued that he could probably train individuals more quickly, because additional training on intelligence gathering and operating in environments with the highest levels of security would no longer be necessary. This suggests that the computer systems used play an important role in driving the content of training and can drive significant variation in the level of training needed.

Job Roles and KSAs

When identifying a training strategy, it is critical to understand the jobs that are being performed and the KSAs that are required to be successful in carrying out the work. The mission and the platform being used are important precisely because they shape job roles and determine the KSAs needed for the job. Our language interviewees noted that the necessary skills extend beyond language skills to include cultural knowledge, such as how to blend in among potential enemies in a foreign country, and technical expertise—for example, many linguists work in cryptology and need strong skills in listening, transcribing, and interpreting. In cyber, a similarly broad set of skills are needed beyond core cyber skills to achieve the highly specialized and complex work that cyber warriors are engaged in.

One of the particular challenges in cyber is that for more highly specialized cyber warriors, job roles are quickly evolving and KSAs are at the cutting edge, so it can be more challenging to identify the KSAs needed to be successful in offensive and defensive warfare. In fact, it is likely that the KSAs needed for offensive cyber warfare are distinctly different from those needed for defensive cyber warfare. Several of the cyber experts noted that while it is important to have foundational skills in computer systems, network structures, and computer programs, these are not the KSAs most critical in effective warfare. Higher-level thinking skills like critical thinking and the ability to recognize patterns are KSAs that distinguish those who are capable of becoming the most effective cyber warriors. Advanced training through the JCAC and NSA training largely focus on developing KSAs related to intelligence, as this is believed to be an important aspect of offensive cyber warfare. One of our experts expressed the opinion that this focus on intelligence was likely important for some offensive cyber warriors but may be less relevant for cyber warriors working outside of the NSA, so the intelligence-focused training may go beyond what is needed and may therefore be inefficient.

The lack of clarity around job roles and the KSAs required for success was a commonly raised issue among cyber experts. However, we noted in Chapter Two that efforts to more precisely define work roles and KSAs are under way, so most of the cyber experts were hopeful that there would be progress in this area soon. For example, NICE has recently made great strides toward defining job roles across the federal cyber workforce and identifying associated KSAs. CyberCom has also been focused on defining job roles and KSAs more specifically for DoD's cyber workforce. Many interviewees expressed a hope that standardized job roles and capabilities would be adopted soon across the services to improve the coordination of training and workforce management. However, well-defined job roles for cyber warriors are challenging to establish, because these job roles are varied, quickly evolving, and at the cutting edge of what is possible in cyber warfare. Given this rapid evolution in specific job roles, it may be prudent to identify the set of KSAs that are needed across a number of the positions and focus on developing those through coordinated training efforts. As several of the experts noted, many of the more specific capabilities that depend on platform or mission may be best developed through on-the-job training by expert mentors who understand the specific KSAs needed in that setting.

In addition to designing training around the KSAs required for certain job roles, it is important to ensure that the training actually delivers in building these capabilities among the workforce. In the language field, testing and certification have played important roles in helping to manage the language workforce. The clear, standardized metrics on which the language workforce is assessed play a valuable role in the ability of DLI and other training organizations to determine what training students need and to measure the outcomes of their students. Similar efforts are under way at CyberCom to develop systems of certifications and assessments for the cyber workforce. However, given that many aspects of technology and cyber warfare evolve rapidly, standardized certifications and assessments may be more challenging to establish and maintain for the cyber workforce than they have been for language.

Training Delivery

While the mission objectives, platform, job roles, and KSAs shape the content of the training, the most effective and efficient way of delivering the training is also an important consideration in building a training strategy. Both language and cyber experts acknowledged the importance of problem-based instruction in training as a means of connecting the skills to the mission and allowing individuals to practice in the setting in which skills will be used. DLI has recently transformed the curriculum to have a larger focus on real-world scenarios. According to one language expert, the ideal way of building language skills quickly is through immersion. However, it is difficult and costly to actually train language students in the countries they will serve in, so DLI creates an immersion-like atmosphere, with long periods of focused instruction with small groups. This was argued by one of our experts to be a real advantage over university-based language instruction, where students have a range of academic and nonacademic distractions. However, university immersion programs and other intensive delivery arrangements may provide a similar opportunity for focus on training in language and cyber.

Cyber experts cited very similar ideals for the delivery of cyber training. They argue that within-DoD training is better able to provide content that is focused on real defense issues and allow individuals to be trained in the cyber environment in which they will work. This is viewed as an advantage over university-based education. However, the CAEs have close partnerships with DoD, so there may be opportunities for university-based students to work in these environments through these partnerships.

Training for cyber warriors is largely delivered through on-the-job experience that is required before and after training courses, and experts argued that this on-the-job experience is critical to effectively building cyber skills. Cyber warfare was argued by our experts to be more like an art form—something that cannot be learned effectively through textbooks and traditional classroom instruction. When asked about the ideal training delivery methods, experts made comparisons to special operations training and/or preparation for a master craft. Students would work closely with an expert mentor and small groups of other students to develop highly specialized skills. To allow for this type of training, experts acknowledged that the workforce management of the cyber field would need to be "rewickered," with a greater focus on training and skill development throughout a carefully structured career path. We discuss the issue of career paths later in this chapter.

Who Is Being Trained?

After identifying the purpose, content, and format of training, it is important to examine who might be trained to understand what gaps in KSAs must be addressed and how training may be best structured to meet the needs of this population. This section describes three considerations that were mentioned by the literature and experts in the language and cyber fields as critical to identifying who will be trained: segment of the workforce, pipeline, screening, and stage of skill development.

Segment of the Workforce

When planning training efforts to meet the capabilities identified, an important consideration is which segment of the workforce— military, civilian, or contractor—can meet these needs, and what jobs these individuals will perform. A 2011 GAO report acknowledged that there was little guidance about the role civilians and contractors should play in the execution of cyber operations, so their roles are currently limited, but they may expand if needs dictate.[2] The estimates of the sizes of each segment are mixed. A 2012 DoD document estimates that the civilian segment of the cyber defense workforce accounts for 78 percent of workers,[3] but an Air Force document from the same year states that there are twice as many active-duty personnel as there are civilians and contractors combined.[4] The same Air Force document predicts an increase in civilian cyber defense workers. However, the experts we interviewed expressed the view that most highly skilled cyber defense workers are typically enlisted personnel. If the workers are civilians or contractors, their training most often comes from outside the military or government. For military enlisted personnel, the training almost always comes from within the military, although it is possible that this may change in the future. Given that DoD has particular control over military training, it has greater authority to ensure that the training is planned carefully, taking into account the specific roles in which the individuals will serve and the KSAs required.

Pipeline

Regardless of job function, the pipeline and recruiting of appropriate candidates is a critical concern to the people we interviewed. The pipeline for cyber warriors and language experts includes both individuals outside of DoD and individuals within DoD who are not currently working in the relevant positions. For language, some attributed pipeline concerns to limited supply of proficient speakers of critical lan-

---

[2]   GAO, 2011b.

[3]   Department of Defense, *Cyber Operations Personnel Report*, 2012.

[4]   Magnuson, 2013.

guages, while others mentioned eligibility constraints—such as requiring U.S. citizenship or requiring a military service member rather than a civilian—that may bar otherwise qualified candidates from certain jobs. According to the interviewees, without an appropriate pipeline, those who manage the workforce are left to train students from zero or very low levels, as is currently the most common case in language. Experts from both cyber and language noted that the pipeline and recruiting challenges for cyber are quite different than those for language. Whereas the experts all commented that language faces a limited pipeline, they expressed the view that the prospects for cyber appear much better in terms of the numbers of individuals with interest, aptitude, or existing skills in the area.

According to the experts we interviewed and sources in the literature, although K–12 language education is growing, the U.S. education system has not yet widely implemented programs that bring an adequate pipeline of second-language candidates to the military. However, they suggested that the situation is more promising for cyber, as there is more widespread acceptance of the importance of STEM education, and more schools have implemented programs that build these skills. Thus, they stated that there are more individuals embarking on military service with a foundation of STEM skills relevant to cyber jobs.

Even with the benefit of the larger pipeline, experts pointed out other challenges. For example, they claimed that the military most commonly attracts individuals who embrace physical challenges, and that cyber does not match those expectations. An expert commented, "The military needs to attract and recruit more geeks, not just the physically strong." Sources in the literature also point out a cultural mindset that undervalues cyber skills as "just IT."[5] Another concern expressed by the experts involves eligibility for security clearances. Experts we interviewed expressed concerns that the most talented hackers might have backgrounds that make them poor candidates for security clearance.

And regardless of the growing number of individuals with STEM skills, an expert suggested that recruiting for cyber warriors should

---

5   U.S. Navy, *Navy Cyber Power 2020*, 2010.

be broad and should draw individuals from less technical fields as well, because those individuals may be talented at the critical thinking needed. The expert commented, "Being successful in cyber is really more about critical thinking, recognizing patterns, and 'connecting the dots.'" Another expert expressed similar sentiments, pointing out that math skills are not the best predictor of cyber expertise and suggesting that further work be done to identify the best predictive factors. Research on hackers supports the idea that hackers "may be born and not made,"[6] reinforcing the idea that training individuals to become hackers may be less promising than recruiting policies that search for naturally talented individuals.

A further and critical recruiting challenge cited by a number of experts was the fact that industry offers greater financial rewards than the military. Interviewees commented that cyber warrior recruitment must find a way to draw those who are passionate about cyber and are attracted to the mission rather than the money.

Screening

According to the experts we interviewed, screening of training candidates is an important step to ensure successful training outcomes and efficient use of funds. As described in Chapter Three, those who manage and train linguist candidates have access to established assessments to measure both aptitude and proficiency (the DLAB and DLPT). Further, language proficiency is measured on a scale common across the military and other government agencies. In cyber, such assessments are not yet established, and although experts widely acknowledge the need to "assess before investing," they described the existing methods for screening as varied and unsystematic. Each service has its own way of identifying candidates, which may be through formal screening or by observing skills on the job. It is important to note that this screening takes place throughout an individual's career in DoD.

Research suggests that screening job candidates for demonstrated competencies could provide several benefits, though research specific to the cyber community is required. It could allow the agencies to

---

[6] Libicki, Senty, and Pollak, 2014.

determine the skills of new workers and plan for training accordingly. It could also allow them to fast-track highly skilled candidates and use their skills immediately. Finally, it could establish targets so that candidates could develop their skills in a targeted way, knowing what will be expected of them.[7]

The experts we interviewed pointed to efforts currently under way or assessments that are being used or piloted on a small scale. They described efforts to test for existing knowledge to make training more efficient. One suggested that cyber move toward a model like the DLPT. That would require a test bank with items to measure both aptitude and skills. However, unlike language, in which the basic content changes little over time, cyber assessment materials must be continuously updated and refreshed. Therefore, if such assessments are to be developed for cyber, there must also be plans for curating the content to keep the assessment valid and current. Assessments would also have to be created for the different areas of cyber expertise.

Because cyber skills are difficult to assess, especially at the higher levels of expertise, some agencies are using alternative methods. One interviewee described an approach in which the top 8 percent of students in an intermediate cyber class were selected to receive further training. Another approach that was suggested was the possibility of on-the-job assessment for the more advanced. Experts pointed out the tradecraft and art of cyber defense and that those skills are difficult to assess through tests but could be assessed through on-the-job observations. According to an expert in the Air Force, individuals typically undergo at least three or four years of screening in a traditional cyber position before becoming a part of the core cyber warfare group. The drawback of such assessments is that they are highly subjective and the outcomes depend as much on the skills of the person making the assessment as they do on the skills of the one being assessed.

Stage of Skill Development

A final consideration with respect to who is being trained is the skill level of the trainees. Over the course of a cyber warrior's career, he or

[7]   Kay et al., 2012.

she will progress through numerous stages of skill development from novice to advanced, and the training needs will differ substantially through the stages. Experts consistently commented that while there may be many options for the more basic foundational training, the more highly skilled and specialized the person becomes, the more the training needs will be tailored to the specific needs of the individual and workforce. This is true in language training, where the common practice is to send all beginners to DLIFLC and to other, more specialized training programs afterward. Then, throughout their careers, they may have access to maintenance resources or further activities to build further skills. Given that training for these specialized workforces happens throughout the career and is highly dependent on prior experiences, it is clear that training cannot be considered outside of the larger system of workforce management. We highlight this in a later discussion of the need to determine how training is integrated into larger workforce management.

For cyber warriors, nearly all interviewees acknowledged a vast variety of options for basic foundational training but commented that the approach to higher-level training must be more carefully planned. Global or foundational training could take place in K–12 education, colleges and universities, and commercial or contractor-delivered training, or through distance learning. One expert suggested that the optimal approach for this stage would be training that is "distributed, asynchronous, and modular," meaning that students could do the training from any location, at any time, and in meaningful units completed at their own pace.

A few experts referred to what happens after the initial global or foundational training as "finishing school" or "topping off" with specialized skills, which may need to be done in a classified environment. A number of experts drew an analogy between highly skilled cyber warriors and "master craftsmen," pointing out that cyber warfighting skills are an art form and that it is important to be side by side with an expert to learn. They suggested apprenticeships or on-the-job training for higher-level cyber skills and suggested that the right candidates would learn quickly in such settings. They also pointed out that higher-level training is better done in person so that individuals and those who supervise them can build trust and mutually establish that an individual is ready for higher-level responsibilities. Further, one expert pointed out the importance of teams in cyber warfighting and suggested that after the initial training, location becomes important. This is the stage at which individuals should be brought to a specific location to work together on real-life scenarios to form effective teams.

What Resources Are Needed?

The previous sections discussed the inputs that shape training, including the capabilities that are needed and the individuals who may help to meet these needs. A third set of inputs that must also be considered are the costs and resource needs. DoD's Cost Assessment and Program Evaluation (CAPE) Office provides a lengthy set of guidelines that must be considered when evaluating the cost and benefit of training.[8] In addition to the costs of the training itself, a range of other costs must be accounted for, including the costs of providing compensation and services to individuals employed by DoD while receiving training. This section describes the issues that were raised in the interviews and literature around these costs and resource requirements, and how they shape decisions on the training strategy for the language and cyber fields. Our experts focused primarily on four aspects of the required resources and costs: the time required, infrastructure and location, staffing, and the cost of delivering the training.

Time

The time required to train individuals is critical to training decisions within DoD. Service members often have limited careers in the military, particularly among the enlisted workforce, which, according to our experts, makes up the largest portion of the highly specialized language and cyber warrior workforces. It is common for enlisted service members to spend just four years in the military, so training must be done quickly to ensure that this expertise provides a return on the train-

---

[8]   See CAPE, home page, undated.

ing investment. Universities have at least four years to train students in specialized fields, but the military does not have this same luxury in training its enlisted forces. The time required to build skills must be balanced against the quality and depth of the training to ensure a sufficient return on investment.

According to our experts and the literature on language training, the time it takes for a cyber warrior or language expert to be trained to the highest levels can be as long as five to seven years.[9] However, as noted previously, it may not be efficient, nor even necessary, to train every cyber warrior to these highest levels. According to one of our experts, it is critical to carefully define the workforce and the skills needed to ensure that training is not provided beyond what is needed for the individual job. By training all individuals to the highest level, training is unlikely to be efficient.

Comments from the interviewees varied as to whether centralized training, service-based training, or university training was most efficient. Some viewed the ability of DLI to train individuals to intermediate skill levels in 24 to 62 weeks as very valuable. One language expert expressed the opinion that "no one could do it as quickly as a central institute." On the other hand, several cyber experts argued that the services are much better equipped to train individuals quickly in highly specialized skills relative to a central training provider. These comments underscored the larger point that different types of training are needed for different types of skills. One expert argued that the services teach people to do tasks as complex as surgery in only six months, so they have a lot of experience with training individuals to high levels of expertise in short periods of time. According to one expert who commented on the CAEs, universities are not yet well equipped to train the most highly skilled cyber warriors and may never be able to provide this training, given the sensitivity of the content. In the case where universities and the military could both provide training, the costs and benefits of training through various outlets can be assessed. Universi-

---

[9]   B. Asch and J. Winkler, *Ensuring Language Capability in the Intelligence Community: What Factors Affect the Best Mix of Military, Civilians, and Contractors?* Santa Monica, Calif.: RAND Corporation, TR-1284-ODNI, 2013.

ties have traditionally taken longer than military-provided training, yet this time is less costly to the government because DoD typically pays a lesser portion of training costs for students at universities and it typically does not pay salaries while enrolled, as it must do while training active-duty military members.[10]

Infrastructure/Location

The need for infrastructure to house training courses and the location of training were mentioned by three of the experts, but infrastructure and location were generally viewed as secondary issues that would not play a major role in shaping the training strategy. If training must be shaped by mission-based experiences and focused on platforms that will be used in the field, these considerations may limit the options for locations. Experts acknowledged some value of gathering people into a single location, including joint team-based training needs and the need to work with a particular set of technical systems. Some language training experts expressed the view that removing trainees from their everyday environments reduced distractions and encouraged focus. However, when other circumstances may make it preferable to keep trainees in their work locations, distributed training is preferred. Several of the experts argued that even centralized training with a single curriculum could be distributed. They further commented that distributed training makes it possible to train greater numbers of individuals.

The services did not report a lack of capacity to provide training in their existing schoolhouses. An expert from the Air Force did report that the need for extensive "hands on" work in intermediate cyber training and the budget environment may limit the overall throughput of students, but the training should be able to accommodate sufficient numbers of students to meet stated CyberCom needs as well as Air Force needs. The Intermediate Network Warfare Training Course

---

[10] It is important to note that DoD does send some active-duty military to universities and continues to pay salaries as individuals attend courses.

graduates more than 7,000 students each year.[11] The military academies are in the process of developing and expanding cyber programs.

Several experts did note the importance of locating university cyber defense programs in colleges nearby military installations to ensure that there is a robust partnership between the Flagship universities and CAEs and DoD. The ability to cycle military experts into university programs to provide defense-specific expertise is important, and the location of the university may impact this. We discuss staffing in greater detail in the next section.

Staffing

Several experts mentioned the importance of acquiring sufficient numbers of faculty with the expertise and willingness to train cyber warriors and pointed to this as a potentially limiting factor. According to language experts, one of the advantages of a central institute model such as DLI is the critical mass of experts. A report on the new CyberCom office cites the value of having a "think tank" atmosphere, with a group of experts coming together to develop innovative training approaches.[12] With regard to allowing the services to provide their own training, several experts expressed a concern that this would constrain the supply of high-quality cyber faculty, because these cyber experts are a limited resource. Another concern was the need to compete with industry for these cyber experts. Yet, not all experts agreed that staffing was a concern. One expert expressed the opinion that the supply of such experts was not particularly limited and that the Air Force, for example, had not experienced problems in that area. One expert commented that the Air Force has aimed to build a culture for its cyber trainers, identifying them as "master craftsmen" and designing a career path that makes teaching more attractive. The expert believed that this approach facilitated staffing and retention.

---

[11] "Digital Warriors: Improving Military Capabilities for Cyber Operations," hearing before the Subcommittee on Emerging Threats and Capabilities of the Committee on Armed Services, July 25, 2012.

[12] Warren Strobel and Deborah Charles, "With Troops and Techies, U.S. Prepares for Cyber Warfare," Reuters, June 7, 2013.

Language experts cited several challenges related to staffing at DLI. Because many of the instructors there are heritage speakers who are not American citizens, they are not eligible to work in environments that require security clearance. Therefore, more advanced mission-based language training that requires a secure environment takes place in other programs after students leave DLI. In cyber, the need for a secure training facility is likely to be even greater. In addition, there were concerns about the ability to cycle in new faculty and new ideas. One language expert noted that when instructors stay at an institution for a long time and "teach as they were taught," their methods can become outdated. Cyber is also likely to face challenges in ensuring that training content remains fresh and cutting edge, given the quick evolution that characterizes cyber work. One expert suggested that one way to ensure an influx of new ideas is to bring in contractors to provide training. Another expert viewed the fact that the services are taking different approaches to cyber training as an advantage because it allows for diverse approaches. However, the same expert suggested that when best practices are identified, some standardization will be beneficial.

A number of language experts commented that working with university faculty is challenging when those faculty are skeptical of partnerships with defense or intelligence agencies, and this distrust can be a major barrier. The cyber experts we interviewed had not encountered similar challenges with contractors and expressed positive views of the contractor responsiveness, based on their experiences. Some cyber experts even viewed contractors as a source of the most current and cutting-edge capabilities, reinforcing the idea that contractors may fill important staffing needs.

Cost

Experts in the language and cyber fields typically focused on the need to ensure that training is as effective as possible. However, they also acknowledged the need to be efficient and ensure a sufficient return on investment on training. This is particularly important in the constrained budget environment that DoD currently faces. The expert interviews focused primarily on the cost of delivering the training to a population of cyber warriors who look similar to today's workforce. They did not consider the implications of shifting the civilian/military mix and did not address the range of other costs that CAPE requires to be considered. Yet, it is important to note that these considerations are important in shaping the costs of training and workforce management. For example, a recent study indicates that it may be cheaper to shift toward civilians as language experts, largely because of the fact that DoD must bear the costs of military training, while civilians are typically trained without DoD resources.[13] Even when civilian training is supported through programs like Scholarship for Service, this support is likely to be less costly, because it does not include the compensation, benefits, and services that the military receives on top of the costs of training delivery. The Congressional Budget Office (CBO) recently recommended that many positions be converted from military to civilian based largely on these differences in cost.[14]

For training provided by the military, there have been concerns about high costs, particularly when the return on investment might be limited by individuals who do not choose to remain in the military. DLI is relatively costly, estimated by two interviewees at more than $200,000 per graduate, though some experts argued that this was a reasonable cost for the high quality of the training and the speed with which DLI prepares the language community. According to the experts interviewed, cyber warrior training is likely to be even more expensive because of the need for expensive, highly advanced computing systems. The need to remain cost-efficient was cited by one expert as an important reason for the CyberCom efforts to identify a clear picture of job roles, KSAs, and associated training needs. This structure will help to ensure that individuals are trained only to the level needed, so that resources are not wasted on training all cyber warriors to the highest level.

---

[13] Asch and Winkler, 2013.

[14] CBO, *Options for Reducing the Deficit: 2014 to 2023*, November 13, 2013, p. 60.

How Will the Training Be Integrated into Larger Workforce Management?

A final important question to consider is how the training plans will be integrated into the big picture of workforce management. We discuss this consideration in relation to four subtopics: retention, management, career paths, and continued training.

Retention

Once workers are trained, organizations must figure out how to get the best return on their investments. This means, among other things, ensuring that workers stay in their positions long enough for the investment to be worthwhile. Experts from both language and cyber raised concerns about retention and the military's "up or out" culture. On the language side, some pointed out that hundreds of thousands of dollars might be invested in a person's training, and the person might leave the service only a few years after. In addition, career growth typically means that responsibilities become more general in scope rather than more specialized.[15]

Similar concerns were raised on the cyber side. Most experts noted that cyber warrior careers do not fit the military well. The Marine Corps and Army were highlighted as organizations that encourage short tenures of three to four years, as opposed to a career of ten years or more, leaving cyber warriors to move into industry or other government agencies. For both language and cyber, a major concern is losing personnel to outside employers. Both groups of workers receive training that makes them attractive to business and industry, which typically pay more than government agencies. The movement of DoD-trained cyber warriors into industry and other government agencies may provide substantial benefits to these entities, though the DoD-specific return on investment will remain limited.

To address competition with industry and other government agencies for cyber warriors, experts pointed to service requirements and such retention incentives as proficiency pay as means to mitigate the

---

[15] Asch and Winkler, 2013.

problem, but they acknowledge that neither is a complete solution. One expert suggested that restructuring careers so that a highly specialized worker can assume a leadership position and continue to pursue work that he or she is passionate about may be a promising way to increase retention. Another suggested that for the most talented cyber warriors, the promise of further advanced training with a corresponding service commitment might help. However, retention incentives may have limited effect on personnel uninterested in long-term tenure. For many individuals, military service is a stepping stone on their career path in that it gives them the opportunity to acquire valuable transferable skills that they plan to take with them to jobs in industry.[16]

Career Paths

A topic closely related to retention is career path. To help retain individuals, career paths should be designed to evolve in a way that allows individuals to continuously build their skills and progress toward increasing levels of responsibility. Experts on language training noted that career paths often do not make the best use of extensive language training, and research on military language professionals suggests considering alternate career paths for these individuals.[17] With respect to cyber, the experts we interviewed noted similarly that military career paths are not structured in a way to retain personnel and leverage the benefit of substantial and costly training. In the typical military career progression, individuals are commonly moved to other responsibilities or exit the service after a few years, which leaves a relatively short time for the organizations to reap the benefits of training investments. Experts also commented that military cyber career paths make poor use of talent by requiring activities for promotion that may be difficult for cyber specialists. They recommended that policymakers first consider how cyber workers in particular build their skills and then design career paths that encourage them to do so. Given the clear incompat-

---

[16]   J. Hosek, M. Mattock, C. Fair, J. Kavanagh, J. Sharp, and M. Totten, *Attracting the Best: How the Military Competes for Information Technology Personnel*, Santa Monica, Calif.: RAND Corporation, MG-108-OSD, 2004.

[17]   Asch and Winkler, 2013.

ibility of cyber careers with existing military career paths, experts suggested a range of possible solutions. These included exemption from restrictions within the existing workforce structure (similar to special allowances made for military physicians) and separation of the workforces within the services (similar to special operations teams). One expert even wondered whether cyber would benefit from becoming a separate service.

The observations from experts and the information from the literature highlight the importance of this concern. Any plans for cyber training will need to take into account how the training fits into the organization's career paths and how it affects retention and career growth. One expert expressed the opinion that without upward mobility in some form, personnel will continue to receive training, reach standards, and then exit the service.

Workforce Management

The topics of retention and career paths flow directly to issues of workforce management, which is the key driver in designing training. Once an individual is trained or if an individual has preexisting skills or talents, his or her supervisors must identify the best way to make use of those skills. Especially for cyber, some experts noted that the services often fail to assign people to positions that best leverage their skills. One expert expressed the opinion that the services are highly inefficient, failing to place the majority of trainees into positions that truly use their skills. The failure may be due to attrition or to individuals being assigned to jobs that have little to do with cyber warfare. Some experts we interviewed also suggested that better use might be made of military reservists and national guard personnel as a way to retain cyber warriors in the military.

Ongoing Training

A final workforce management issue to consider is continued training, which is a concern for nearly every area of expertise. For language professionals, ongoing maintenance is essential. It is typical for military linguists to be required to do language maintenance activities, with specific hours of training given. They may also be tested annually with the DLPT to ensure that they have retained or enhanced their skills as needed. The need for continued training for cyber warriors is equally important but different in nature. While the content of language expertise changes little over time, cyber knowledge and skills are continuously changing. What is current today will become outdated quickly, and cyber personnel, especially those at higher skill levels, must be aware of and able to work with the latest technology.

For cyber warriors, continued training is doubly challenging because not only must individuals be given training, but training must also be continuously developed and updated with an eye to the future. Both activities require substantial investments and must be planned carefully.

Summary

In this section, we provided a framework for understanding the range of different issues that must be considered in developing training. We highlighted a number of areas in which language and cyber face similar challenges, as well as some clear differences. In the areas where cyber faces similar challenges, language may offer some preliminary lessons learned that can be used to inform policy around cyber training and workforce management. In the final section, we highlight these potential lessons learned for cyber.

CHAPTER FIVE

Preliminary Lessons from Language Training for Cyber Training

DoD faces substantial challenges in meeting the needs for the highly skilled cyber warrior workforce. The quickly accelerating demand for cyber warriors, the substantial time needed for training, and the challenges with managing and retaining the workforce raise concerns about shortfalls in meeting the needs for offensive and defensive cyber operations. This exploratory study focused specifically on the question of training and what might be learned by the cyber field from defense language training. We relied on expert interviews from the cyber and language training fields in the government and postsecondary institutions and a review of the literature to identify parallels in efforts to quickly train individuals for highly skilled positions. Similar comparisons could be made between cyber and other fields, such as special operations, or others that involve specialized skills.

Through our interviews with experts and review of the literature, we found a number of common issues confronted by cyber and language training. For example, the need to align training with mission needs, train personnel quickly to perform at high levels, and screen individuals who have an aptitude for the particular skill are key issues in both the cyber and language fields. We developed a framework to represent the overarching set of considerations that emerged in the interviews across both fields as recurring themes important to strategic training decisions. We used these considerations to organize our discussion of more-specific questions, such as whether to develop a central institute for cyber warrior training versus pursuing service-specific or university-provided education and training.

There are some preliminary lessons that can be drawn from language to inform the training and workforce management of the cyber warrior workforce. Based on an overview of the defense language training landscape, our review of the literature, and insights from experts in both language and cyber training, we identified several themes that policymakers and planners should consider for the training of cyber warriors:

- **Shared definitions, training standards, and metrics are an important first step in ensuring efficient training and workforce management.** They give diverse stakeholders the ability to share a common vernacular, set goals, and assess outcomes consistently across the field. Defense language training benefits greatly from the existence of established skill-level descriptions and tools to measure aptitude and proficiency. In cyber, a number of efforts are under way to establish shared definitions and metrics for the field. When they become widely available, they will be important assets to those who plan and design training. However, given that many aspects of technology and cyber warfare are rapidly evolving, standardized certifications and assessments may be less useful to the cyber warrior workforce than they have been for language.

- **Close alignment with mission needs is important to effective training.** In language and cyber, as in any domain of national security, mission needs may vary substantially. Training is most effective and efficient when it is well matched to the responsibilities of the individual in his or her service to the mission, whether it is a joint or service-specific mission. For example, in language training, personnel may attend a government or civilian institution for foundational training, but more advanced and job-specific training is accomplished through specialized training programs, such as the National Cryptologic School for cryptologists or CIA University for intelligence analysts. Those advanced training programs exist to address specific mission needs. Regardless of the delivery mode—whether it is through an institution, agency, or contractor and in person or remote—the training must be aligned with the anticipated job responsibilities of the learner and the overall mission of which the job is a part. As a result, training for service-specific cyber missions may look very different from joint training that is focused on national cyber warfare issues.

- **Training may benefit from a variety of training providers and delivery methods to enable responsiveness to diverse mission needs and diverse groups of trainees.** Defense language training comes from many sources. Some individuals may enter military or government service with preexisting skills. For many who do not, DLIFLC serves as a joint resource for global language and culture skills training, and the services, other government agencies, universities, and contractors provide further training in higher-level and mission-specific skills. For cyber, a number of experts pointed to the advantages of distributed, modular training for some skills; in-person, on-the-job mentorship for others; and team-based training for others. Their comments point to need for a variety of options to meet diverse needs.

- **Training individuals from a zero skill level is costly and often inefficient, so building a strong pipeline of candidates may be beneficial.** As numerous experts noted, language training can be expensive. Advanced cyber training similarly requires substantial time and resources. However, experts in both language and cyber pointed out that the amount of training required is substantially reduced when candidates come to their jobs with existing expertise. While there may be a somewhat larger pipeline of individuals with an interest in cyber relative to language, the skills that are required to achieve the highest levels of cyber expertise are less prevalent. Therefore, the field may benefit greatly from efforts to cultivate the pipeline to increase the pool of candidates with critically needed skills. Those individuals may still need further mission-specific training, but it is likely to be less resource-consuming if the individuals come to their jobs with a baseline of skills.

- **Cyber training may benefit from the development of validated screening tools or processes that can be used across**

the field. Because not everyone will be successful even if trained, experts identified aptitude screening as an important mechanism to identify the most promising candidates. This may be particularly true in the cyber field, where the pool of individuals is larger, and those qualified to reach the highest levels of expertise may be a small portion of the total pool. Although experts acknowledged the shortcomings of existing language aptitude measures, language training has benefited from stakeholders' ability to screen candidates for aptitude. A number of cyber experts cited a need for aptitude screening for the larger cyber workforce as well. They described the potential usefulness of assessment-based screening to channel talented individuals into the larger cyber workforce, and the use of long screening windows of more than three years to identify the most promising candidates to become cyber warriors. Aptitude screening in cyber may look very different from that for language, but if the field can develop appropriate screening tools or methods, it may substantially ease the burden on training by identifying those who have the potential to reach the highest levels of expertise.

- **Alignment between workforce management priorities and training plans is important.** Because advanced skill training is so costly and time consuming, those interviewed emphasized that stakeholder agencies will benefit from planning that takes into account the need to develop career paths and workforce management approaches that aid retention and most effectively leverage the workers' skills. For the language field, interviewees expressed concerns about the retention rate of language trainees because many of those who receive substantial and expensive training leave the workforce within a few years of completing it. Given that advanced cyber training (including screening through job experience) was reported to take as many as six years, and highly skilled cyber workers are attractive to private industry, the experts interviewed highlighted the importance of identifying ways to retain these individuals. They suggested that service commitments and the opportunity to be at the forefront of cyber warfare may be important tools to aid retention. However, they expressed the view that additional efforts to improve career paths and work-force management will facilitate even greater returns on these substantial training investments.

Besides these key considerations, this exploratory study high-lights the larger point that while defense specializations may differ in many ways, there may be substantial overlap in the issues they face. For cyber, a field that is steadily growing in importance, with a workforce that is not yet defined well or fully understood, there is an opportunity to learn from other defense fields. Language professionals are just one example. It will be useful to conduct similar studies of fields that have parallels to cyber, such as medical fields or special forces.

With the cyber landscape changing continuously, cyber war-rior workforce needs are likely to change at a corresponding pace. The framework and key considerations described in this report can help policymakers plan training carefully and effectively.

References

Alexander, General Keith B. (Ret.), Commander of United States Cyber Command, "Statement Before the Senate Committee on Armed Services," March 27, 2012.

———, "Statement Before the Senate Committee on Armed Services," March 12, 2013a.

———, "Cybersecurity: Preparing for and Responding to an Enduring Threat," Statement to the Senate Committee on Appropriations, June 12, 2013b.

Asch, B., and J. Winkler, *Ensuring Language Capability in the Intelligence Community: What Factors Affect the Best Mix of Military, Civilians, and Contractors?* Santa Monica, Calif.: RAND Corporation, TR-1284-ODNI, 2013. As of September 7, 2014:
http://www.rand.org/pubs/technical_reports/TR1284.html

ASVAB, home page, undated. As of August 21, 2014:
http://official-asvab.com/

Blank, Steve, "Flying High: Why the Military Is Taking Cyber Warfare Seriously," *Forbes*, April 29, 2013.

CAPE—*see* Cost Assessment and Program Evaluation.

CBO—*see* Congressional Budget Office.

Clapper, James R., Director of National Intelligence, "Worldwide Threat Assessment of the U.S. Intelligence Community," Statement for the Record: House Permanent Select Committee on Intelligence, April 11, 2013.

Congressional Budget Office, *Options for Reducing the Deficit: 2014 to 2023*, November 13, 2013. As of April 30, 2014:
http://www.cbo.gov/budget-options/2013/44765

Corrin, A., "Is There a Cybersecurity Workforce Crisis?" *FCW*, October 15, 2013. As of August 21, 2014:
http://fcw.com/articles/2013/10/15/cybersecurity-workforce-crisis.aspx

Cost Assessment and Program Evaluation, home page, undated. As of September 8, 2014:
http://www.cape.osd.mil/

Defense Language Institute Foreign Language Center, "Command Language Program Support," undated.

Defense Language Institute Foreign Language Center General Catalog, 2011–2012. As of August 21, 2014:
http://www.dliflc.edu/publications.aspx

Defense Science Board, "Resilient Military Systems and the Advanced Cyber Threat," Task Force Report, January 2013.

DeKeyser, Robert M., "The Robustness of Critical Period Effects in Second Language Acquisition," *Studies in Second Language Acquisition*, Vol. 22, 2000, pp. 499–533.

Department of Defense, "Joint Terminology for CyberSpace Operations," Memorandum for Chiefs of the Military Services, Commanders of the Combatant Commands, and Directors of the Joint Staff Directorates, 2010.

———, "Strategy for Operating in Cyberspace," January 2011a.

———, "Cyber Operations Personnel Report," Report to Congressional Defense Committees, April 2011b.

———, *Cyber Operations Personnel Report*, 2012.

"Digital Warriors: Improving Military Capabilities for Cyber Operations," hearing before the Subcommittee on Emerging Threats and Capabilities of the Committee on Armed Services, July 25, 2012.

DoD—*see* Department of Defense.

Foreign Service Institute, *Language Continuum*, Arlington, Va.: U.S. Department of State, 2004.

Fryer-Biggs, Zachary, "DoD Still 3,700 Cyber Experts Short of Full Staff," *Defense News*, April 25, 2013.

GAO—*see* U.S. Government Accountability Office.

Gould, Joe, "Army Ramps Up Cybersecurity Skills Training," *Army Times*, November 19, 2012. As of September 21, 2013:
http://www.armytimes.com/article/20121101/NEWS/211010319/Army-ramps-up-cybersecurity-skills-training

Gould, Joe, "Be an Army Hacker: This Top Secret Cyber Unit Wants You," *Army Times*, April 8, 2013.

Grosjean, F., "Bilingualism's Best-Kept Secret: How Extensive It Is," *Psychology Today*, 2010. As of August 21, 2014:
http://www.psychologytoday.com/blog/life-bilingual/201011/
bilingualisms-best-kept-secret

Hosek, J., M. Mattock, C. Fair, J. Kavanagh, J. Sharp, and M. Totten, *Attracting the Best: How the Military Competes for Information Technology Personnel*, Santa Monica, Calif.: RAND Corporation, MG-108-OSD, 2004. As of September 8, 2014:
http://www.rand.org/pubs/monographs/MG108.html

Hussey, E., and J. Novick, "The Benefits of Executive Control Training and the Implications for Language Processing," *Frontiers in Psychology*, Vol. 3, 2012.

Interagency Language Roundtable, "An Overview of the History of the ILR Language Proficiency Skill Level Descriptions and Scale by Dr. Martha Herzog," undated[a]. As of August 21, 2014:
http://www.govtilr.org/skills/IRL%20Scale%20History.htm

———, "Descriptions of Proficiency Levels," undated[b]. As of August 21, 2014:
http://www.govtilr.org/skills/ILRscale1.htm

Kay, David J., Terry J. Pudas, and Brett Young, "Preparing the Pipeline: The U.S. Cyber Workforce for the Future," Institute for National Strategic Studies, August 2012.

Language Flagship, "The Flagship History," 2012. As of October 1, 2013:
http://www.thelanguageflagship.org/content/flagship-history

Language Flagship, home page, 2013. As of October 1, 2013:
http://www.thelanguageflagship.org

Libicki, Martin C., David Senty, and Julia Pollak, *Hackers Wanted: An Examination of the Cybersecurity Labor Market*, Santa Monica, Calif.: RAND Corporation, RR-430, 2014. As of January 20, 2015:
http://www.rand.org/pubs/research_reports/RR430.html

Magnuson, Stew, "Air Force Cyber-Operations Wing to Go on Hiring Binge," *National Defense Magazine*, January 17, 2013. As of September 24, 2013:
http://www.nationaldefensemagazine.org/blog/Lists/Posts/Post.aspx?ID=1026

Michaels, Jim, "Pentagon Expands Cyber-Attack Capability," *USA Today*, April 23, 2013.

National Initiative for Cybersecurity Education, homepage, 2014. As of September 6, 2014:
http://csrc.nist.gov/nice

National Security Agency, "List of Centers of Academic Excellence for Cyber Operations," 2014.

National Security Education Program, "Language Training Centers," 2013.

NICE—*see* National Initiative for Cybersecurity Education.

Novick, J., E. Hussey, S. Teubner-Rhodes, J. Harbison, and M. Bunting, "Clearing the Garden-Path: Improving Sentence Processing Through Cognitive Control Training," *Language and Cognitive Processes*, 2013.

NSA—*see* National Security Agency.

Panetta, Leon, Memorandum, OSD 09206-11, August 10, 2011.

Pellerin, Cheryl, "For Navy, Cyber Has Inherently Military Operational Aspect," *American Forces Press Service*, June 12, 2013.

Project Go, "Program Overview," 2013.

Rhodes, N. C., and I. Pufahl, *Foreign Language Teaching in U.S. Schools: Results of a National Survey*, Center for Applied Linguistics, 2010.

Rivers, W. P., and E. M. Golonka, "Third Language Acquisition Theory and Practice," in M. Long and C. Doughty, eds., *The Handbook of Language Teaching*, New York: Wiley-Blackwell, 2009.

Ryan, C., *Language Use in the United States: 2011*, U.S. Census, 2013. As of August 21, 2014:
http://www.census.gov/prod/2013pubs/acs-22.pdf

Serbu, Jared, "DoD Building Cyber Workforce of the Future," Federal News Radio, September 9, 2012. As of September 11, 2013:
http://www.federalnewsradio.com/885/3021032/
DoD-building-cyber-workforce-of-the-future

Skorton, D., and G. Altschuler. "America's Foreign-Language Deficit," *Forbes*, August 27, 2012. As of August 21, 2014:
http://www.forbes.com/sites/collegeprose/2012/08/27/
americas-foreign-language-deficit

Starks, Tim, "Facing Up to the Nation's Shortage of Cyber-Warriors," *Roll Call*, March 19, 2013.

Strobel, Warren, and Deborah Charles, "With Troops and Techies, U.S. Prepares for Cyber Warfare," Reuters, June 7, 2013.

U.S. Army Cyber Command, "U.S. Cyber Command Conducts Tactical Cyber Exercise," *Sound Off!*, undated.

U.S. Army Garrison Presidio of Monterey, "History of the Defense Language Institute Foreign Language Center," last updated January 10, 2013.

U.S. Department of State, "Foreign Service Institute," undated.

U.S. Government Accountability Office, "DOD Faces Challenges in Its Cyber Activities," Washington, D.C., GAO-11-75, May 2011a.

————, "More Detailed Guidance Needed to Ensure Military Services Develop Appropriate Cyberspace Capabilities," Washington, D.C., GAO-11-421, May 2011b.

U.S. Navy, *Navy Cyber Power 2020*, 2010.

U.S. Navy, *InfoDomain*, Virginia Beach, Va.: Navy Cyber Forces Public Affairs Office, Summer 2013.

United States Code, Title 10, Volume 3, Armed Forces, 112th Congress, House of Representatives, July 2011.

Witte, Brian, and Dan Elliot, "Air Force Academy Training Cadets for Cyberwarfare," *Standard-Examiner*, April 26, 2013. As of September 12, 2013 http://www.standard.net/National/2013/04/26/Air-Force-Academy-training-cadets-for-cyberwarfare.html